What peopl

"This book, which is written with great sincerity, is Will McVicar's way of looking at and interpreting A COURSE IN MIRACLES. It is a book for those who wish to uplift their spirit and let go of fear."

Gerald G. Jampolski, M.D.,
Author of LOVE IS LETTING GO OF FEAR

"Will McVicar has captured some of the major teachings from A COURSE IN MIRACLES in an easy to understand fashion. It will be a comfort to those who are troubled by the materialism and turmoil of modern life."

Dorothy H. MacRae, Science of Mind, Prn.

The words of Will McVicar express the elegance of his passion and conviction as Will explores his rising awareness of "The Sons of God." For many, the words of Will may touch present awakening through the heart of this wonderful work. I personally feel the beauty of the Comforter, felt the Oneness, rising from these pages as obstacles melt into Harmony.

Ed Mayer
Devotee of the Course and Juris Doctor

THE SONS OF GOD

Teachings from *A Course in Miracles®*

WILL MCVICAR

LOVE PUBLISHING

THE SONS OF GOD

Teachings from *A Course in Miracles®*

by WILL MCVICAR

Published by:

LOVE PUBLISHING
P.O. Box 611
Indiantown, FL 34956

First edition 1997

Library of Congress Cataloging-in-Publication Data
McVicar, Will
THE SONS OF GOD
LCCCN 97-94089

ISBN 0-9658888-1-9

ACKNOWLEDGMENTS

To my children, Hedy, Billy, Greg, Cindy and Barry from whom I learned the meaning of love. To my wife Dorothy, who showed me there is a purpose to this life.

Cover by Michael Visconte,
Florida's Competitive Edge, Stuart, FL.

PREFACE

In the fall of 1987 I bought a small motor home and went looking for a nice warm place to spend the winter. I had taken early retirement from a career in computer system design and looked forward to a refreshing change in lifestyle. I ended up on Cudjoe Key in the Florida Keys where I pursued my interest in things metaphysical.

During WWII I had an out-of-body experience while on convoy duty in the North Atlantic. From then on, I was hooked on the metaphysical world. Key West is near Cudjoe and is a marvelous place for such pursuits. Before long I was enrolled in a class in *A Course in Miracles®*. Up to this point I had read most of the books by or about Edgar Cayce, Jane Roberts and Shirley MacLaine, plus various works on spiritualism and related subjects. I had also read some books on comparative religions.

But nothing had prepared me for the grandeur of the philosophical concepts in the Course. I do not have a religious upbringing so words like God, Holy Spirit, Christ, Atonement, the separation and elder brother were not part of my normal lexicon.

The Course enthralled me. I have been a student ever since. It has changed my entire outlook on life. I am now a happy person though I was a jaded cynic before. There is little in this life that can give me much concern now – even that dark specter death holds no fear for me. This remarkable attitude is shared by many of my fellow classmates.

The author of the Course calls himself our elder brother. To my surprise, halfway through the Course he tells us that we are now teachers of God. This bothered me for a long time until I finally decided to write this book. The language of the Course is often quite poetic and beautiful. But some of the concepts are sometimes abstract and difficult to comprehend. As a result, much class time is spent in discussions seeking a simpler explanation of the text. Also, many students dropped out of the Course because they had difficulty following the abstract nature of many of the passages.

This book is couched in the language I use to teach the ideas I found in the Course. The message of the Course is so inspiring that it should be made available to everyone. It is my hope that those who read this book will go on to further study of *A Course in Miracles*® and find the same peace I have.

I have approached this work with reverence and love. I dedicate it to all my fellow seekers of the truth.

Will McVicar

Indiantown, FL

TABLE OF CONTENTS

		Page
Chapter 1	**LIFE ON PLANET EARTH**	1
	Introduction	1
	The World We See	2
	How It All Starts	3
	Falling in "Love"	4
	What is This thing We Call "Love"?	6
	The World of Illusions	7
Chapter 2	**WHY WE FEEL GUILTY**	11
	Introduction	11
	The Belief in Sin	12
	The Holy Spirit	14
	The Atonement	15
	Time is an Illusion	17
	The World We think We Live In	18
	How the Ego uses Guilt	20
	Transcending the Ego	22
	Look Within	23

Chapter 3	**ALL ABOUT SIN**	25
	Introduction	25
	The Ego's Religion	26
	The Role of the Body	30
	The Role of the Holy Spirit	32
Chapter 4	**THE BODY**	37
	Introduction	37
	The Ego and the Body	39
	Removing the Blocks to Healing	41
	Escape From Prison	44
	A little Ship	47
	The Body is an Idol to the Ego	48
	Let Us Use Our Reason	52
Chapter 5	**OVERCOMING FEAR**	57
	Introduction	57
	The Beginning of Healing	58
	Miracle Minded Thinking	61
	Fear is a Call for Love	64
	Keep No Secrets From the Holy Spirit	67
	Sacrifice is Not Love	70
	The Holy Spirit's Messengers	73
	The Fear of Death	74
	Miracles Will Overcome Fear	77
	Waking From the Dream	79
	Choose Heaven or Hell	81

Chapter 6	**THE REAL WORLD THROUGH FORGIVENESS**	83
	Introduction	83
	Learning About Forgiveness	84
	Listen to the Holy Spirit	86
	The Real World	90
Chapter 7	**THE HOLY INSTANT AND THE HOLY RELATIONSHIP**	95
	Introduction	95
	The Holy Instant	96
	Elder Brother in the Holy Instant	98
	The Conditions For Love	100
	A New Look at Relationships	102
	The Holy Relationship	104
Chapter 8	**IT TAKES TWO**	111
	Introduction	111
	We Are Our Brother's Savior	112
	No One is Special	114
	Healing By Joining	117

Chapter 9	**ACCEPTING THE ATONEMENT**	**121**
	Introduction	121
	How healing is Achieved	122
	The Altar of God	127
	Unity through Christ	131
	Our Brother is Our Savior	134
	The Little Space	135
Chapter 10	**THE LIGHT WITHIN**	141
	Introduction	141
	Let Our Brother's Light Shine	141
	The Vision of Christ	145
	Spreading peace Through the Sonship	147
	The Mirror of the Mind	152
	Heaven in the Holy Relationship	156
	Returning Home at Easter	158
	The Power of Love	161
	We Are One in God's Will	163
	Walk Beyond the Darkness To the Light	165
	We Stand on Holy Ground	168
	When We Wake Our Brother	171
	The Light is in Each of Us	173

Chapter 11 THE FINAL JUDGEMENT 175

Introduction 175
Some Answers 176
What's It All About? 176
Why Am I Here? 177
What Am I? 179
Is There a Better Way? 181
What is Love? 182
What is death? 185
What is Life? 189
The Last Judgement 191

Epilogue 194

Chapter 1

LIFE ON PLANET EARTH

Introduction

Everyone on this world is seeking the elusive goal of happiness. From the time when we first become aware that we can influence our own destiny we start looking for things; events, encounters or relationships with others that we think will make us happy. Some accumulate wealth and/or power, believing that their happiness lies in the accumulation of material things or control of people and events. Some seek fulfillment through the pursuit of special relationships.

Many find a kind of happiness helping the poor and needy with various charities. There is a kind of ecstatic happiness when one achieves a difficult goal, such as climbing a mountain, solving a difficult puzzle, a religious experience such as communion with God, or helping another overcome a physical or mental problem. There are many ways in which we experience an episode of unrestrained joy.

But after the ecstasy of the moment, vague doubts set in to plague us. During our normal, working day there are very faint, nagging thoughts that there must be a better way to spend our life than in the drudgery of everyday on the job. As the poet says: "It's a work-a-day world in which we live, where we get mud on our boots."

Very faintly, somewhere in the back of our mind, we yearn for the innocence we think we have lost. Some try to ignore their sadness in games they play to divert their attention from the fact that they are sad. The popularity of games such as golf and tennis or watching professional sports are good examples of how people can delude themselves into thinking they are happy by keeping their thoughts occupied with trivia. We follow these pursuits to hide the part of our lives that is missing from our consciousness.

There is another way of looking at the world. Our conventional ideas of what we are and where we are, are all wrong. We have taught ourselves that we live in a body and inhabit a planet which we call the earth. The proof of these ideas is fed to our brains in a continuous stream of information from our five senses. But these ideas are all false. Our true nature is the reverse of these beliefs and is described in this book.

What you are about to read will give you a new perspective on this life. You will learn why we are here, who we are, what this world is, where we come from and where we are going. The message is one of hope and peace and joy. It will help you in your quest for truth and peace, so please keep an open mind and heart as you read on. We are embarking on a journey inward in quest of our true Selves.

The World We See

Everyone begins to wonder, at some time in their life, about the nature of this world we think we live in. Unpleasant things frequently happen to people and they start to believe that life isn't fair. They are quite right, life is not fair. Marriages end in divorce, couples can no longer live together and so they break up, neighbor argues with neighbor and country fights with country.

Crime runs rampant on city streets. The modern trend in housing is to build developments with gated entrances so the security police can keep undesirables out. As people get older, their bodies become susceptible to many different ailments and diseases. No one seems to escape some form of torment.

Those who are "successful" and accumulate material wealth are not happy. They come to understand that material things do not bring happiness. They eventually realize they share the same road as the most miserable person alive. All roads on this world lead to the same place – death. Questions regularly pop up about our existence here. In our more thoughtful moments, as we wander from crisis to crisis, we ask ourselves questions like these:

What's it all about?
Why am I here?
What am I?
Is there a better way?
What is love?
What is death?
What is life?
Answers will be found in this book

How it all Starts

When we were first attracted to another person, strange urges and longings coursed through our body. We were strongly attracted to the other, spending enormous amounts of time, energy and, later in life, money, in the pursuit of their favors. Sometimes we were successful and satisfied our desires. But when we did, we found there was no satisfaction, only a fleeting pleasure. We began to realize, because of the lack of satisfaction, that there must be something more to life – that better way.

But most don't give up. They keep pursuing the "impossible dream." As they progress through the various stages from child to youth to adult, they may have many affairs. Nothing seems to be permanent or enduring.

Some few stay with the same mate for their entire lifetime. But their road through life is not always smooth and thornless. They continually have to make compromises to remain together. Even the best intentioned couples have arguments and hurt each other. They end up staying with each other more for convenience than for any other reason. They just cannot be bothered to overcome the inertia of a lifetime of the habit of living together.

Falling in "Love"

When we were in the hormone hurricane of high school we usually fell madly in "love" with an attractive person. But what was it we fell in "love" with? Was it a pretty face, a nice body, bulging biceps, broad shoulders, or some other physical characteristic?

It was the outward appearance – the form of the person – that we were attracted to. As we got to know the other we

---

"Married in haste, we may repent at leisure.--"
William Congreve: The Old Bachelor

learned whether or not we really liked the person inside the form – the content. In most cases we were willing to compromise whatever reaction we had to him so we could stay next to the other's body.

The relationship based on physical attraction usually leads to marriage or some other form of coupling. But there are many things on which they disagree. The disagreements lead to argument. So about half of the marriages end in divorce. Other forms of a relationship also end in failure for similar reasons. It seems that a tranquil, loving relationship between two people is impossible. Using outward appearance as the selection criteria, it should be obvious that the odds against this kind of relationship must be astronomical.

And so it goes. We wander through life, lurching from relationship to relationship, as we constantly change our goals. We follow our "natural instincts" which, as has been shown, lead to unsatisfactory results. Those who stay together in a committed relationship make many compromises. They could hardly be called unconditionally happy. So they keep looking for that better way. We feel that we are not in charge of our own destiny, but are at the mercy of forces beyond our control.

Why is this so?

The problem is, we are attracted to form regardless of content. We base our judgement on outward appearance rather than on the true worth of an individual. This ridiculous lack of good sense is the cause of most of our problems in all fields of

---

"Oft expectation fails, and most oft there
Where most it promises."
William Shakespeare: All's Well That Ends Well

human endeavor where inter-personal relationships are involved, such as everyday encounters at work, play and home.

We spend large amounts of time and money on improving our physical appearance so we will be more attractive to others. We are blinded to the inner person by what we see with the body's eyes. But we do not spend any time learning what we should be doing to find the peace and joy that can come from the right relationship.

What is This Thing We Call "Love"?

What we felt for that special someone was not love, it was infatuation, or, more properly, lust. It was a desire to possess their body as our own because we thought we lacked something that they had and we could gain by the relationship. Our better judgement was suspended in the pursuit of the other as we schemed for their favor.

And we had additional unpleasant feelings to compound our imagined bliss. At the same time as we were professing our love there was a sub-conscious urge to attack that we were not aware of. But it was there. It made us feel vaguely guilty for reasons that we could not understand. In our thoughts we noticed a peculiar phenomenon. When we thought of our loved one there seemed to be a secondary, unpleasant thought about him which underlay our main thought. We were not imagining this. It actually happened. The Orwellian double-think really does happen, and it happens all the time.

" The web of our life is of a mingled yarn, good and ill together."
William shakespeare: Alls Well That Ends Well

At the slightest provocation these secondary thoughts burst upon our conscious mind and, before we knew it, we were expressing them in a very loud voice. After the argument was over, we wondered where these unpleasant thoughts came from. We felt they were not expressing our real feelings. And we were right, they were not.

They were coming from a part of the mind that we will call the ego. All of the negative emotions such as hate, fear, lust, envy, anxiety, malice, jealousy, etc., come from the ego. They are the opposite of love, which stands alone, but with great power, against them and is our true nature.

We are capable of only two emotion, love or fear. All of the negative emotions are just different manifestations of fear. Fear and love cannot coexist. At times these negative emotions seem to govern our actions. They seem to overpower our sense of reason. We let them take over our thoughts and actions, making our life miserable. But they can be overcome. This book will show you how to change and choose that better way that will lead to complete happiness.

The World of Illusions

This is how it all came about: God created us as His one Son. He gave all His power to us to share with Him. He gave us everything in the universe as His perfect Son. He gave us free will but, exercising our free will, we decided we wanted special favor. In that instant this world, where we could be separate from the Father, was born.

This world is not what we think it is. It is a world of illusions, peopled by shadows that seem to lead lives full of pain, sorrow and despair. But it is all in our minds. There is nothing outside of us. We are constantly making up the external world we see as we make our way through life, fearfully trying to avoid the dangers we think we perceive. Our minds are so powerful that we constantly write the script for everything that seems to happen to us. We think we are a body that slowly ages and dies. We believe everything our five senses report back to us.

But what if our senses reported back to us only that which we sent them out to find? What if our minds were all joined and our smallest thoughts affected everyone? What if our brother agreed with our concept of what we are and we agreed with his concept of what he was? Then, given the power of our minds, we could be anything we wanted to be. What if our mind was powerful enough to make any kind of world we wanted to be in? Then we could do what we thought we really wanted to and behave any way we pleased.

In reality our minds are powerful enough to move mountains, because faith, coupled with belief can accomplish anything we set our minds to. We are constantly co-making this world we think we live in. It was made as an attack on God. It symbolizes fear because it is based on fear. Everything here is an illusion. Those who choose to come here are seeking a place where they can be illusions and avoid their own reality. It was made to be a place where God could not enter, where His Son could be separated from Him.

Perception was born here. Our eyes and ears report back to us a dream world. We made them to support the illusions we want. They go out to find what the mind has ordered them to

---

"The inaudible and noiseless foot of Time."
William Shakespeare: All's Well That ends Well

seek. But our sight can be redirected, our ears can be trained to hear a different song and our perception given a new purpose so we can escape from the world we made.

There are two levels for our thought systems. The body, or lower level, *makes* the physical world. The spirit, or higher level, *creates* the spiritual world. Both levels are foundations for belief systems by which one lives. But they are mutually exclusive. One cannot live partly by one set of beliefs and partly by another. As a child of God, our mind has the power to make a powerful thought system. The lower level – the body – is the prison we have made.

Each individual makes his own private world with his own forms of fear. He alone perceives the sights and sounds of this private world. Only he is aware of this insanity. The population of his world consists of figures from his past. They are not real because they are made from his reactions to his brothers. But they do not include his brother's reactions to him. He does not see that his private world is different from other private worlds. His figures are not whole, lacking the loveliness of the Son of God. They are perceived in his mind only.

In our private world we are sleeping. We see in darkness what we made. Our eyes are closed yet we think we see because we have denied vision. Vision is entirely different from seeing. Denial of vision means we accept insanity. We believe we can make a private world in which we decide what we can see.

Think of us as children dreaming of a make-believe world populated by our imagination. We like to see wars fought and watch disasters happen. Like a little child we want to keep our parent out of our world so we can do naughty things without being punished. We feel guilty about this but hide the guilt and indulge ourselves in terrible events such as earthquakes, hurricanes, wars, famine, floods and drought.

We have chosen to create differently than God so we are fearful. We are not at peace because we are not fulfilling the lofty function He gave us. That is why we have these vague feelings of being unfulfilled and dissatisfied with our lot in life. Our function here is to forgive ourselves and our brothers. This incredible situation is only an unbelievable dream. It is inevitable that we will wake up and return to God.

"The self is not something that one finds – it is something one creates." Thomas Szasz

Chapter 2

WHY WE FEEL GUILTY

Introduction

Have you ever wakened in the morning with a vague sense of guilt and wondered what you did to justify feeling that way? You are not alone in this feeling of vague uneasiness. Everyone has felt that way at some time in their life and most feel that way every morning. There is a reason for it.

All of us experience guilt at some time but very few realize why. The mind is a very powerful instrument. When a thought is combined with a belief, the surge of power can literally move mountains. The mind never sleeps and is always creating. We do not believe this, not because it would be arrogant, but because we are afraid of our thoughts. We do not respect the mind's power because our concept of it is ridiculously inadequate.

There are never any idle thoughts. Every thought produces form at some level. The mind does not reside in the body's brain as is commonly thought. The brain holds the body's memories and controls its actions. But the essence of you, what you really are, is not in the brain. It is in the mind. The mind co-makes the world we think we see. We are constantly co-making with everyone else. Each mind contains all minds and all minds are joined. The mind is constantly showing us what we think we want to see.

In the creation, God created us as perfect, lacking nothing. He gave us the ability to create with Him. We can and do misuse our ability to create by projecting our thoughts on the canvas of this world. We do this because we believe there is some lack in us that we can fill using our own ideas.

We believe the following:

- Our mind can change God's creation.
- The perfect can be made imperfect or lacking
- We can distort God's creations, including ourselves
- We can create by ourselves and head off in our own direction.

None of these distortions existed prior to the separation, and actually do not exist now. But we think they do because we let ourselves be governed by the voice of the ego.

The Belief in Sin

The ego believes we have usurped God's power. It believes it is our essential self. If we identify with the ego, we will experience guilt and be fearful of punishment. The idea of attacking God is the insane idea we believe when we listen to the ego, a tiny part of the mind. We believe we have torn part

---

"There are more things in heaven and earth,
Horatio,
Than are dreamt of in your philosophy."
William Shakespeare: Hamlet

of Him away. The resultant guilt is so strong it must be projected outward by us onto our brother in an attempt to get rid of it. We are relieved by this but our brother seems to be our enemy now.

Our mind will accept as real whatever we *choose* as reality. When we feel guilty it is our natural belief in sin. Sin is only a lack of love. As soon as we perceive sin correctly – as an error – then we will act positively to remedy the situation because no one likes to leave an error uncorrected. We will be successful because this will give us the freedom that we subconsciously are looking for.

The healed mind – with all guilt gone – is sane and heals the body because it cannot conceive of illness. The ego believes that by punishing itself, i.e. making the body sick, it can blunt the punishment of God. It gives to God the intent to punish and then takes this intent as its own choice. This is obvious insanity and shows the ego is completely mad.

The ego interprets the Laws of God according to what it wants. We constantly answer the question, "What do I want?" Our decisions, based on what our answer is, are judgements that have definite effects on this world. There are only two choices open to us; the Holy Spirit or the ego. One was created by God so we cannot eliminate it. We made the other, so we can. Our delusional ideas about what we want are not real thoughts, our real thoughts are buried beneath the ego's raucous shrieking.

We usually believe in our ideas about what we think we want so they have a strong influence on our actions.

The Holy Spirit

The instant we wanted special favor and became separated from God, He placed His Answer, the Holy Spirit, in our minds. The Holy Spirit is in all minds, constantly guiding us on the road back to God. He is our conscience, the still, small voice of reason. He is the way in which God's Will is done on earth as it is in Heaven. He is our communication link with God. When we talk to Him we are talking to God. When He talks to us, it is God talking.

> **Holy Spirit** - the Christ Mind which is aware of the knowledge that lies beyond our perception. He came into being with the separation and will stay with the Sons of God after the Atonement is complete. Who are the Sons of God? *We* are the Sons of God. The Voice of the Holy Spirit is the call to the Atonement.

The Holy Spirit is the shared inspiration of all the Sonship. He induces a kind of perception which contains many elements found in the Kingdom of Heaven:

- It is universal and sharing.
- It involves only gain.
- It points the way beyond healing.
- It is incapable of attack and does not obstruct knowledge in any way.

Guilt feelings are a sign we believe we think separately from God, and that we want to. Guilt is inescapable to those who want to be in control. They believe they are responsible for their errors. This is irresponsible thinking. Our responsibility is to accept the Atonement for ourselves.

The Atonement

Atonement - a chain of events consisting of forgiveness and miracles. When complete it will change perception to true vision, the ego will be undone and we will not be separated from the Father. The purpose of the Atonement is to make us realize we already have everything and to save the past in purified form only.

All fear is based on the thought we can usurp God's power. When we accept the Atonement we will escape from fear because we will know that our errors never occurred. Atonement means undoing – as in the undoing of fear. The miracles' part in the Atonement is the undoing of fear.

The effects of our wrong thinking – i.e. the world full of misery we think we see – can be undone. Our guilt feelings are caused by our continuing decision to remain separated from God. If we decide to accept the Atonement for ourselves then we will see a different world, full of happiness.

Guilt feelings maintain the idea of time because the anxiety produced ensures that the future will be like the past. The ego encourages this because this is how its continuity is guaranteed. We can escape from the domination of the ego by accepting God's continuity of eternity. When we make this change we will exchange time, guilt, viciousness and pain for eternity, joy, love and peace.

Elder brother - author of *A Course in Miracles®*. When he was a man, he was known as Jesus of Nazareth. He is in charge of the Atonement. His role is to set our will free. The ego will oppose him in every way possible.

The Atonement is the natural occupation of the children of God. Whenever we offer forgiveness or a miracle we will experience a feeling of well-being because we are fulfilling our function in this world. Our elder brother stands at the end of the Atonement waiting to undo all errors that we could not correct. He is in charge of the Atonement and we will become part of it when we are restored to our natural state – the Sons of God. We will join him in his crusade to correct error when we are ready and willing to use our own power to work miracles.

We feel guilty because we think we have been treacherous to God. The Holy Spirit dispels guilt as part of His teaching. Our guilt feelings come from listening to the ego's voice which tells us we deserve death because of our treachery. Confusing ourselves with the ego, we begin to think we want death. We believe, wrongly, that death comes from God, not from the ego.

First we condemn, then we attack and then we feel guilty. The mind has judged another as deserving punishment, not love. This causes a separation where one mind sees itself as separate from another. It believes it can escape punishment by punishing another. The mind deludes itself by denying what it is. It does not want to rid itself of the denial, but to keep it and look for sin in this world. Our denial of our true Selves has hidden the Father from us. It has driven us insane.

Time is an Illusion

Time is a device the ego uses to perpetuate its existence. It is an illusion. Time goes backward to an ancient instant that is beyond our remembering, but because it is an instant, time is constantly relived, over and over again. It seems to be the present, the *now* we are experiencing. We continually relive this ancient instant that hides eternity from us.

Every instant of every minute of every day we relive the single instant when the time of terror took the place of love. We die each day to live again until we cross the gap between the past and present. It is not a gap at all. Each life is a seeming interval from birth to death and then on to life again. It is a repetition of an instant long gone that cannot be relived. Time is only the mad belief that what is over is here and now.

Guilt feelings maintain the idea of time because the anxiety ensures that the future will flow directly from the past, and be just like the past with no present time in between. The ego encourages this and thus maintains its continuity.

The only part of time that is real is *now.* The past is gone and the future is yet to be. We try to maintain the continuity of time by our belief the future will be like the past. The present moment, the *now,* is an instant of time that flows directly into eternity, this instant and every instant. Every instant, taken together, is eternity.

When we look at what we think are our past deeds and thoughts, we may wonder how we can be guiltless. Our "sins"

"Thus the whirligig of time brings in his revenges."
William Shakespeare: Twelfth Night

occurred in the past in time, not in eternity. But there is no past. When we reach the end of time and look back at the past, it will roll up like a long carpet behind us and disappear. If we believe the Son of God is guilty then we will walk along this carpet in a long, miserable and senseless journey to death.

Everyone is trying to escape the prison he made. The release is in each of us, we will find it in time, even though time is only an illusion. The Son of God is still as God created him. He is guiltless, his purity forever shining in God's Mind. We have buried the understanding that we are immortal. But we live in eternity, not in time. Guilt ensures the continuity of the ego, but our continuity is guaranteed by God, not the ego.

The World We Think We Live In

The separation began the instant guilt was accepted into the mind of God's Son. It will end with the acceptance of the Atonement. In that instant we asked for special favor and the strange world we made rose in the black cloud of guilt we accepted as ours. The Son of God "sinned" and became invisible.

> **This world** - a delusional system of madmen driven insane by guilt. It is the symbol of punishment. Its laws are the laws of death. Children are born in pain and through pain. As they grow, they suffer. They learn about sorrow and separation and death. They think their mind is in their brain and its power is diminished if

---

The world 's a bubble, and the life of man
Less than a span. Francis Bacon

the body is harmed. They think they love and yet they seem to lose what they love – an insane belief because love cannot be lost. In the end the body withers away and is interred in the ground. They think God is cruel for subjecting them to this.

This world of guilt demands that love has to kill to save and that attack is salvation. Only the guilty could conceive of this insanity. Adam believed it was the Father Who drove him out of paradise. So he lost the knowledge of the Father. The Apostles misunderstood that the crucifixion was a call for peace because their own imperfect love made them vulnerable to projection. They spoke of the "wrath of God" because they were afraid. But God is a loving Father Who would never harm His children. Their sense of guilt made them angry about the crucifixion. The crucifixion followed by the resurrection is proof there is no death.

The Holy Spirit wants to remove all guilt from our minds. He wants to make himself unnecessary by teaching us all He knows. The Father can be remembered only in the peace that will come when all guilt is ended because peace and guilt are opposites. Love and guilt cannot exist at the same time, they are mutually exclusive. Christ is hidden from us when we feel guilty. Guilt declares that God's Son is full of blame.

Christ - the Son of God. He lives in His Creator and shines with His glory. He is the extension of the Love and the loveliness of God. He is as perfect as His creator. He is at peace with Him.

As soon as we have accepted the Atonement for ourselves, we will see God's Son as guiltless. If we look upon him as guiltless we will know his oneness with us and with the Father. Guilt comes from condemnation, which leads to separation. We can condemn only ourselves. When we do, we lose the knowledge that we are God's Son. He was created out of Love and he lives in love. He extends the Love of his Father. Goodness and mercy have always followed him wherever he goes.

We can change our feelings of guilt. Only the ego can feel guilty so if we change our mind about those our ego has harmed, the Atonement can release us. Let us leave the "sins" of the ego to our elder brother, that is what the Atonement is for. When we do, we will experience the happiness God wills for us.

How The Ego Uses Guilt

The ego's purpose is fear. Only the fearful can be egotistical. Heaven and earth are both in us and our mind can side with either. Let us choose Heaven as our goal. The ego is the symbol of separation, and the symbol of guilt. Guilt is always disruptive, the symbol of attack on God.

When we have accepted the Atonement we will learn the past has never been and the future is yet to be. While we think we are in time the future is identified with doing penance. Only guilt could induce this sense of an unfulfilled need. Let us accept the guiltlessness of the Son of God as our own because we are the Sons of God.

The ego's plan to dispel guilt is to make it real and then atone for it. It believes in the insane notion that attack is salvation and will lead to atonement. Holding guilt dear, we share this belief with the ego. The ego teaches us to attack ourselves because we are guilty. But attack makes us feel guilty, so the vicious circle is complete and there is no escape.

We project our thoughts outward to get rid of our guilt. But the ego wants to retain the guilt. The part of the mind that is right-thinking finds this intolerable because it knows that this stands in the way of our remembrance of God, Whose pull is so strong we cannot resist it. The ego insists we are guilty so we cannot be ourselves. This splits our mind between God and the ego, causing insanity.

We are actually concealing the guilt when we project it onto our brother. We still feel the guilt but we do not know the reason why. The ego claims we have failed a weird array of its "ideals." Believing we are no longer Sons of God, we are failing to be ourselves. The Holy Spirit teaches us to recognize that guilt has never occurred. Without guilt attack is impossible. He knows the guiltless Son of God cannot attack himself.

Hidden in a dark and secret place in our mind lies the realization that we have condemned God's Son to death. The ego wishes to destroy the Son of God because it sees him as a threat to its existence. It does not know who the Son of God is because it is blind. If it perceives guiltlessness anywhere, it will try to destroy it because it is afraid. We do not even suspect this insanely murderous idea is there, hidden in our mind.

The ego holds the strange belief that the guiltless are guilty. It tries to make them feel guilty in any way it can. It believes that those who do not attack it are its "enemies." If we disagree with its understanding of salvation, we are in an excellent position to let it go. Let us look upon this dark secret so we can dispel the ego by not attacking our brother. The ego cannot shield us from the truth, which is that we love our brother.

Our guilt comes from a secret belief that we have sacrificed God's Son. The wish to kill has hidden him from us. We are afraid to find him because we would still wish to crucify him. We have controlled this wish to kill ourselves by not knowing who we are – by identifying with the ego. But, make no mistake, the ego does want to torment and destroy us.

The crucifixion is the symbol of the ego. The ego attempted to kill the Son of God because of its strange belief guiltlessness is blasphemous of God. The ego believes it is God and any guiltlessness is the final guilt that must be punished with murder.

Transcending the Ego

The ego is undone when we are released from guilt. But when we make someone fearful we also feel his guilt. The ego punishes those who obey its harsh commandments. Faithfulness to the ego is rewarded with pain. When we condemn a brother we are teaching him he is right in his delusion of guilt. To believe the guiltless Son of God can attack himself and become guilty is insane. Sin and condemnation are the same. Belief in one is faith in the other.

Faith is rewarded in the terms of the belief in which the faith was placed. Where faith is invested determines what the reward will be. Faith is always given to what is valued and what we value is returned in kind. The world will give us what we value. We are constantly projecting it, so what we find is what we have placed our faith in. If we value darkness then we will not be able to see. The future will be like the past if we have placed our faith in the past.

The Atonement forces us to re-evaluate our concepts of what is true or false. We have elevated guilt and innocence as both being true. We do not believe the Son of God is guiltless when we see a brother's past instead of his present. If we choose to condemn a brother we continue to feel guilty ourselves. If we do not condemn him, but see him as sinless instead, we free him from the past. In doing this, we have freed ourselves. What we do to our brother, we do to ourselves because we are all one with each other.

To be free of guilt, we must see no one as guilty. Let us accept the Holy Spirit's offer of Atonement for all our brothers and it will be true for us. We cannot condemn the Son of God in part. If we see anyone as guilty, we will see guilt in ourselves. Guilt is always present in our minds. When we project it, it cannot be undone.

Look Within

The world seems dark to us, shrouded by the cloud of guilt we projected. We cannot look within because we are afraid of what we think we would see. But what we fear is gone. If we look within we will see the Atonement, shining in peace and quiet. The ego tells us not to look within because we are black with guilt. It tells us to see the guilt in our brothers as that will absolve us. This keeps us blind to the light within. God placed the light that is shining there. Let us not be afraid to look. We will find that what we feared to look at has been placed there with love.

When guilt touches a relationship, the person is avoided so the guilt may be avoided. Real relationships are holy, to be used by the Holy Spirit. When we try to unite with anyone for our individual salvation, the Holy Spirit cannot use the relationship for our release. Salvation must be shared to be real.

When we try to make a brother feel guilty, we will feel guilty. Those who suffer guilt try to displace it unto others. They do not look within and let it go. They do not understand love because they see the source of guilt outside themselves.

Let us look inward and we will see that the source of our guilt is not there because the past is not in us. In this world we find no real relationships because we let our weird associations with the past stand between us and our brothers. Let us seek a relationship wherein we join with a brother for the purpose of learning the Holy Spirit's lessons.

We do not see our brothers as they really are because we try to use them to "solve" the past. We did not want salvation in the past so we cannot use our brothers to solve problems that are not there.

We have made a world in which we think we lack things. Before the separation God gave us everything, and we have not lost it, it still is ours. We think we have deprived ourselves by setting up a set of false needs. These needs are established by our self-concepts – the ego. We can find peace only when we want to learn about complete forgiveness.

Chapter 3

ALL ABOUT SIN

Introduction

The Son of God has betrayed himself, his brothers and his God only in his dreams. His "sins" are only in his imagination. He needs to be awakened, not forgiven. What he has dreamed has not really happened. It has no effect on reality. Our minds will accept as real whatever we *choose* as reality. If what we choose makes us feel guilty it is because of our unnatural belief in sin.

The belief in sin is a lack of love. Sin would be irreversible if it were possible in reality. The belief that minds, not bodies, can attack is the basis for the belief in sin. When we have erred, this should not be confused with sin. Error can be corrected, whereas sin calls for punishment. The belief that punishment corrects anything is insane. The concept of punishment involves the projection of blame, but no one is punished for the belief in sins and the Sons of God are not sinners.

The belief in sin is the arrogant idea that to sin is to successfully violate reality. It assumes the Son of God is guilty, making of himself what God did not create, and that creation is not eternal. It assumes the Will of God is open to opposition and defeat. It is the grand illusion beneath the ego's grandiosity. By it God Himself is changed and incomplete.

The Ego's Religion

The Holy Spirit will never command us to obey His wishes. This would assume inequality and the Sons of God are all equal. We obey laws that are other than God's because we made them. If God showed us the insanity of this, it would show we have not sinned. Because we are part of God, God cannot lose His own certainty. What we teach, we are, and God cannot teach that we have sinned. If God showed our true Self to the little self we made, we would be fearful and doubt the sanity of our mind.

Our problem is we do not try to control our thoughts since we believe our thoughts are private and cannot harm anyone. But this is wrong. Our mind is part of God's and as such we share it with everyone. There are no idle thoughts, every thought creates form on some level. Our task is to learn to control our wandering thoughts and realize how important they are. Within us the Peace of God is shining, waiting for us to choose to look upon it.

The rewards for this are great. We can see the world we choose to look upon. Instead of seeing a world of hate and attack, we will see a world of mercy and love.

We have not sinned but we made a mistake when we denied God. Like a little child acting contrarily, we denied God because we loved Him. We knew that if we recognized our love for Him we could not deny Him. Therefor, we really do love Him and we know that He loves us. The memory of this is hidden in our mind. These thoughts are our real thoughts that we think with God.

He created us wholly without sin or suffering of any kind. If we deny Him then we bring pain, sin and suffering into our mind. With the power He gave it, our mind is capable of creating worlds. But it can also deny what it creates because of our free will.

The Son of God cannot sin. He can be mistaken, deceive himself, or even turn the power of his mind against himself. But he cannot change his reality in any way or make himself guilty. Sin would do that. But sin is impossible. The wages of sin is death and the immortal cannot die.

In the ego's insane religion sin is not error but truth, and purity is arrogance. It teaches that accepting the self as sinful is holiness. This doctrine replaces the reality of the Son of God as His Father created him. It is the ego's attempt to keep creation hidden from truth by keeping it separate.

If we try to reinterpret sin as error the ego will use every defense at its disposal to counter this thinking. The ego teaches that the idea of sin must be approached with reverence and awe. It is the most "holy" idea in the ego's thought system; true, lovely and powerful. It is the ego's armor; the fundamental purpose of special relationships.

The ego made its world based on sin. It is an upside down world where the thinking is reversed from reality. Its seeming solid foundation is simply clouds of guilt that seem to be heavy and impenetrable. In it sin has changed creation from an idea of God to an ideal the ego wants. It is a world of bodies that it rules. They are mindless and capable of complete corruption and decay. This is nothing more than a mistake which can be undone easily by truth.

If we bring any mistake to be judged by truth then it can be corrected. But if we give it the status of truth then everything is brought to it for judgement. This is how the "holiness" of sin is kept in place. But it is impossible to have faith in sin because sin *is* faithlessness. Let us bring it to truth, for it is a mistake. If we have faith that it can be corrected then we can be confident it will be.

The idea that sin is real is the most heavily defended in the ego's arsenal. It believes that sin is the natural expression of what the Son of God has made himself to be. Such is the ego's reality, the "truth" from which escape is impossible. It is what the Son of God is, his past, present and future. He has corrupted his Father and changed His mind completely. The ego's wish is the death of God, Whom sin has killed. It believes it has accomplished this in its madness.

All this is nothing more than an easily corrected mistake. Its correction is as simple as walking through a heavy fog into the sunshine. If we are tempted to agree with the ego that it would be far better to be sinful than mistaken, we must be very careful before we make the final choice. We are choosing between Heaven and hell.

The mind will not let the idea of sin go while the attraction of guilt is found in it. Sin will always be desirable. We try to repeat it because we like it. The sin may never be acted out to its final conclusion because our fear becomes very strong. We will always desire it as an essential part of what the ego thinks we are. The ego thinks it is impossible for sin to call upon love, which always answers. It thinks sin always calls upon fear, and demands punishment. It believes punishment preserves sin. We want what we think, in our madness, is real and we are reluctant to let go.

We always try to correct what we see as error because we do not like what is not attractive. Sometimes we can repeat a sin time and time again with distressing results but it does not lose its appeal. However, if we change its status to a mistake then we will not repeat it. But if the guilt remains, then we have changed only the form of it. We have acknowledged it was a mistake, but it is still uncorrectable because guilt is still there. We have not really changed our perception of it.

The Holy Spirit recognizes and would correct mistakes. But He cannot punish sin because it is meaningless to Him. Mistakes call for correction because they are a call for love. Sin is only a mistake we want to keep hidden, an unheard call for help.

The Son of God can make mistakes in time. The Holy Spirit sees this and so do we. But we do not share His recognition of the difference between time and eternity. While we believe in sin the Holy Spirit cannot teach us time is a tiny part of eternity. If we listen to the Holy Spirit's teaching we can see time differently and see beyond it. Error can be corrected by the mind, but sin is the belief our perception cannot be changed. If the mind does not accept what it perceives through the body's eyes, the mind is judged insane. Therefor, the only power that could change perception is kept helpless.

If sin is real, then we are not and God is not. The Creator extended Himself in creation. What is part of God cannot possibly be different from the rest. If sin is real then God must have created part of Himself that is at war with the rest. He must be split, partly sane and partly insane. He must have created what wills to destroy Him. Is it not easier to believe we have been mistaken than to believe this ridiculous argument?

The Role of the Body

We believe in sin as long as we believe anyone's reality is restricted to a body. Our belief that bodies can unite keeps guilt attractive to us. The belief that the mind is limited to the body leads to the perception that separation is everywhere. God and His creations seem to be overthrown and what God created holy cannot stand before the power of sin. Can this be reason or is it madness?

To the ego sin means death so salvation is achieved by the Son of God being killed instead of it being destroyed. But no onc can die for another. Death does not atone for sin. We can live to show sin is not real. While we believe the body can get us what we want it appears to be the symbol of sin. If we believe it can bring us pleasure then we will also believe it can bring us pain. To believe we could be satisfied with so little asks pain to fill our skimpy storehouse, making our life complete. Guilt creeps in where happiness has been removed.

The ego has dedicated the body to the goal of sin. Its disciples continuously chant the body's praises, celebrating the ego's rule. Everyone must believe that yielding to the attraction of guilt is the escape from pain. Everyone must regard the body as himself, without which he would die. But within it, his death is equally inevitable.

If we see a brother's body then we are judging him, not really seeing him. We are imagining him in the darkness of sin. Truth is kept hidden by illusions in our imagining. We are picturing our brother's reality as a body in unholy relationships with other bodies. He serves the cause of sin for an instant and then dies.

The body's eyes adjust to sin. They see it everywhere, in everything. Everything stands condemned by our judgement when seen through them. Because of the power of our mind we will see what we want. We see a painting of attack by everything on everything on the canvas of the world. A fearful world is projected if the goal is sin. We uphold it by adjustments we do not realize we have made. We spend huge amounts of energy in maintaining this picture.

Sin is a limit and whom we limit to a body, we hate because we fear them. We have condemned them to a body by our refusal to forgive them. The practices of sin are dear to us so we place our faith and belief in the body. If we saw our brothers as sinless then holiness would set him free by removing fear – and therefor hatred – at its source.

Sacrifice is always demanded of a body by another body. The mind tries to use the body to carry out the means for sin in which the mind believes. Those who value sin believe in this joining of mind and body. Sacrifice is thus a means for limitation, and, therefor, for hate.

The Holy Spirit will correct errors without making anyone fearful. He will never teach us that we are sinful. We are afraid to look within and see the sin we think is there. The ego smiles in approval at fear in connection with sin. It does not doubt our belief and faith in sin. But when we overcome our fear and look within we will begin to see the light shining there. The ego will try to obstruct our efforts by using all the power we gave it when we made it.

The part of our mind that uses reason cannot see sin. It can see errors and this will lead to their correction. It tells us that when we think we sin, we are really calling for help.

We cannot accept or refuse correction without our brother. Sin will try to convince us that we can. Reason will tell us that we cannot look upon a sinless world and see ourselves as guilty. Neither can we see a sinful world and not be part of it. Sin maintains we must be separate. But reason tells us we cannot have private thoughts if our minds are joined. Thoughts that enter into our mind must have an effect on other minds.

The cost of sin is to be helpless. All our misery comes from the belief we are powerless. Everyone knows the Son of God is not powerless. Therefor, those who see themselves as helpless must believe they are not the Son of God. They join the hordes of the powerless and envy their brother's power, unaware they already have everything. They are afraid of it and make him their enemy. Those who look on sin deny seeing the real world which is all around them.

The lonely and alone are the only ones who need sin. They see their brothers as different, making the need for sin seem justified. An unholy relationship is one where each one thinks the other has something that he does not have. They each try to complete themselves by coming together and robbing the other. They stay together long enough to think there is nothing left to steal. Then they move on. They wander through a world of strangers that are different from them. They live in their bodies under a common roof that shelters neither. They live in the same room and yet are a world apart.

Nothing can be secret from God's Will. We believe we have a secret "will" apart from His. Reason will tell us this is a mistake, not a sin. We should not let our fear of sin protect it from correction. Reason sees through it because it is an error. It can see the difference between sin and mistakes.

The Role of the Holy Spirit

Belief in sin requires a lot of defense at enormous cost. Everything the Holy Spirit offers must be defended against and sacrificed. Sin is carved out of a block of our peace, and laid between our brothers and ourselves where it blocks the road to peace. No one would try to pass by it without the help of reason.

Every sin and every condemnation we perceive and justify is an attack on our Father. That is why it cannot be real. We think the Father and the Son are separate because of our fear. So it seems safer to attack another or ourselves instead of the Creator, Whose power we know.

Specialness is the idea of sin made real. Sin arose from a base of nothingness – the ego. This "creator" made the Son different from his father. There are many "special" sons. Each one is in exile from himself and from his Father. They chose specialness instead of Heaven. They wrapped it in sin to keep it safe from truth.

We have made sin with the form of specialness cherished by us – the body. We defend it with all our puny might against the Will of God. It is our enemy, not God's. It seems to make us separate from God when we defend it. This idol that seems to give us power has really taken it away. We have given our brother's birthright to it, leaving him alone and

---

Reputation, reputation, reputation! Oh, I have lost my reputation! I have lost the immortal part of myself, and what remains is bestial.
William Shakespeare: Othello

unforgiven. We stand in sin beside him, both of us in sadness before the idol that cannot save us.

The Holy Spirit can commute each sentence we laid on ourselves, so they cannot be sins. Sin is the only thing in this world that cannot change, being permanent. The world depends on its changelessness. The world's magic seems to hide the pain of sin from sinners. It deceives with glitter and guile. But each one knows the cost of sin is death. Sin is a request for death, a wish to make this world's foundations as sure as God Himself. The world is safe from love to everyone who thinks sin is possible.

The Father and His Son are made co-creators by the agreement of their thought. But if the Son chooses to believe one thought opposed to the truth, he has decided he is not his Father's Son. Now he believes the Father and His Son are insane. We believe this when think anything in this world is sane. It does not matter what form it takes. Sin is not real because the Father and Son are sane. The world is meaningless because it rests on sin.

What is not love is sin. Each of these sees the other as insane and meaningless. Sinners perceive a world based on love as wholly mad. They believe theirs is the way to sanity. Love looks on sin as being insane. Sinners see justice as their only punishment. The laws of sin demand a victim. It does not matter who it may be, for the cost of sin is death and must be paid. This is insanity, not justice, in a world where justice is defined with insanity.

Those who still believe sin is meaningful find it hard to understand the Holy Spirit's justice. They believe He cannot avoid the vengeance their confused idea of justice brings. They fear the Holy Spirit. They perceive the "wrath of God" in Him.

They believe He can strike them dead with bolts of lightning torn from the "fires" of Heaven by God's Own angry Hand. They believe Heaven is hell. They are afraid of love. When they are told they have never sinned, suspicion and fear come over them. Their world depends on sin for its stability. They perceive the "threat" of God's justice to be more destructive to them and their world than vengeance, which they understand and love.

They think the loss of sin is a curse and flee from the Holy Spirit as if He were a messenger from hell, sent to work God's vengeance on them, disguised as a deliverer. They think He is a devil dressed in an angel's guise. They think He offers no escape for them except a door to hell, disguised as Heaven's gate.

It is arrogance to think our little error cannot be undone by Heaven's justice. We think they are sins, not mistakes, not correctable and to be met with vengeance, not justice. If we keep and hide our little problems they will become our secret sins.

Anything in this world we believe is good, valuable and worth striving for can hurt us and will. Not because it has the power to hurt, but because we have denied it is only an illusion and made it real. It is real to us. Through its perceived reality all the world of sick illusions has entered. All belief in sin, in power of attack, in hurt and harm, in sacrifice and death has come to us. No one can make one illusion real and escape the rest. We cannot keep one illusion we prefer and still find safety in the truth.

The Son of God can never sin. But he can wish for what would hurt him. He has the power to think he can be hurt. This is a false perception of himself. It is a mistake, not a sin, and is forgivable. He needs help, not condemnation. Is it our purpose that he be saved – or damned? What we choose him to be to us will make our future. Let us make our choice *now* and in this instant all time will become a means to reach our goal. The purpose of the world we see is chosen in this same choice.

The Holy Spirit has use for all the means for sin we made. Because His purpose lies in the opposite direction, He uses them to lead away from sin. We made perception so we could choose among our brothers and seek for sin with them. The Holy Spirit uses perception to teach us that the vision of the holy relationship is all we need to see. When we have learned this lesson, we will give all our faith to holiness. We will believe in it because that is our desire.

"We must learn to live together as brothers or perish together as fools."

Martin Luther King, Jr.

Chapter 4

THE BODY

Introduction

The body is the symbol of what we think we are. God did not make it, we did. It is a device we made so we could be separate from our Father. We made it so we could pursue sin with our brothers. It does not exist in reality. The Holy Spirit will take the body and translate it into a learning device when we ask Him to. The mind, being very powerful, can heal the body but the body cannot heal the mind.

The purpose of the body is to help us return to our original state of direct communication with the Sonship and our Father. Under the Holy Spirit's guidance it becomes a learning device that will be needed no longer when the lessons have all been mastered. Two choices are available to us; a loveless empty shell – the body – or miraculous channels of communication – the mind.

True communication is between minds. When we are able to establish it , separation will be brought to an end. But we have to be careful not to attack because this promotes separation. The body is beautiful or ugly, peaceful or savage, helpful or harmful depending on how we use it.

We are all God's children. He created us the good, the beautiful and the holy. While our vision is dim here on earth we can still use the body to express the love of God and learn to change our perception to vision.

The physical senses perceive the body as a means for attaining "atonement." This is a fantasy of a mind gone out of control. The body is actually a defense against the Atonement. Perceiving the body as a temple is the beginning of the realization that, no matter how beautiful, the body really does not exist. The only reality is the inner altar which spiritual sight will show us when we overcome the fear of the Atonement and look within.

The body is a ncutral part of this world. When we accept this truism, we cannot deny the body exists. If we do, then we are denying the body is a manifestation of the mind's fundamental power. In addition, we are denying the power of the mind itself.

The mind can cause the body to act wrongly. The mind can believe, erroneously, that the body is capable of creating. This is the cause of all physical symptoms. The belief that matter can create is a belief in magic. Only the mind can create and it cannot create beyond itself. The only use for the body is a training device for the mind under the Holy Spirit's guidance.

The body is the learning device, the mind is the learner. It can be an obstacle to learning if we attach any significance to it. The mind can be filled with light and can begin to regard the body for what it is when it realizes the mind, not the body, is the learner.

We made the body so we could have something to perceive with and something to perceive. This has induced a conflict in the mind. To resolve it, we try to interpret the body as our real Self. But the body represents a huge loss in power. This alienates us from spirit. We perceive spirit as a threat, but spirit, being knowledge, does nothing.

The Ego and the Body

Our thoughts operate on two levels. The body thoughts, or lower level, make the physical. The spirit thoughts, or upper level, create the spiritual. Both levels are foundations of belief systems by which one lives. As a child of God, the mind has the power to make a powerful thought system. The lower level, the body, is the prison we have made.

The ego does not believe in equality, only inferiority and superiority. It needs to confirm its existence by acquiring both what the body needs and so-called "higher ego needs." It believes the body is its home and tries to satisfy its needs through the body. Therefor, physical appetites are not of the body but of the ego. This confuses the mind about what is really possible in this world, the physical or the spiritual.

The ego chooses the body, which it hates, as its home. It tells us the body's vulnerability proves we are not of God. It tells us the mind is part of the body, which cannot protect it. The mind, being dazed, tries to find a safe haven for protection. When the ego tells it to look to the ego for protection, the mind reminds the ego that the ego's home is the body, so it offers no protection. The ego's response is to obliterate the question from the mind, which causes a vague uneasiness in the mind.

The ego believes part of the mind is against it. It feels justified in attacking its maker. It senses the presence of the Holy Spirit, but they do not exist on the same level so it can have no direct awareness of Him. The ego turns to the body for an ally. But the body is not part of the Son of God. The compact that is formed is one based on separation and fear.

The ego uses the body to attack the mind. It tries to persuade the mind that it, the mind, is the ego's learning device and the body is more real than the mind. But the mind is real and the ego is not. Anyone who listens to and believes the ego, is not in his right mind. The ego develops the body's abilities so it can act independently and alone. The Holy Spirit develops only the body's communication ability so healing can occur.

The Holy Spirit teaches that only the mind is real because it is shared. The body is separate, not part of us. To be of one mind is meaningful, but to be of one body does not mean anything. Therefor, the body is meaningless. The Holy Spirit sees the body as a means of communication only. He translates communication into being. Communication, being sharing, becomes communion.

The ego uses the body for attack, pleasure and pride. Promoting fear promotes attack and attack always breaks off communication. Egos join in temporary allegiance for what each can get separately. The Holy Spirit teaches us to communicate with our brother only what we can give to all.

The ego teaches we are a body and therefor our function is to attack. The body's health depends on our interpretation of

---

"Men fear death as children fear to go in the dark; and as that natural fear in children is increased with tales, so is the other." Francis Bacon its function. In perception the whole is the sum of the parts but in knowledge, to know in part is to know the entirety. The part and the whole are the same because each part contains the whole, so one brother is all brothers and each mind contains all minds.

The ego tries to teach us the body can communicate and create so it is self-sufficient. But only minds communicate so the ego tries to teach us the body can act like the mind. The lower, or body level should not be used for either teaching or learning since we can act contrary to what we believe. We would be weakened as a teacher and learner because we would teach both sickness and healing.

Removing the Blocks to Healing

The Holy Spirit will teach us to use the body as a device to remember who we are. Knowing this, the Sonship will be re-unified in our minds. But if we try to use our own judgement instead of His, the body will be used improperly. This always leads to hatred, attack and loss of peace.

We look on the body as having many different functions in this world. Guided by the ego it appears to be ruled by chaos. This will all be changed if we let the Holy Spirit be our guide. Then the split part of our mind that is wrong-minded will return to spirit. The body will become a temple where devotion to the Holy Spirit will replace our slavish devotion to the ego. In this sense, it will become a temple to God. His Voice will remain with us, directing the use to which the body will be put.

If the mind thinks the body is real, it will distort the way it perceives the body, and the result will be illness. The mind always controls the health of the body. It blocks its own normal extension beyond the body, perceiving the body as a separate thing. The removal of these blocks is the only way to guarantee help and healing.

When we see a brother as a body, his power and glory are "lost" to us, as are ours. But loss of any kind is impossible to the Son of God. The body is not a limit. Whenever we see another as limited to or by the body, we are dictating this limit to ourselves. This is wrong because our whole purpose in learning is to escape from limitations. If we believe attacks can give us happiness, we have not learned the Holy Spirit's lessons.

The world seems to nag the body with two different voices. The body shifts from one guide to the other, confusing concepts of health and sickness. The ego makes the fundamental mistake of regarding the body as an end in itself. Every end the ego has urged us to accept has not satisfied us when it was reached. As a result, we are constantly changing our goals and we end up living a life of "quiet desperation" with a vague sense of not being fulfilled.

The ego has a heavy stake in sickness because that proves we are vulnerable and, therefor, not the Son of God. Being vulnerable, we feel we must attack to protect ourselves. But we are only attacking our own invulnerability. By recognizing this, we can give up attack and withdraw support for the ego. This negates the ego's most powerful weapon against us.

The body's true function – communication under the guidance of the Holy Spirit – is obscured because the ego establishes the body as an end in itself. The body is not for sickness, it is neutral. Sickness becomes meaningful when two of the ego's premises are true. These are: the body is for attack, and we are a body.

The ego constantly asks questions but only the Holy Spirit knows the answer to everything. When we are tempted by the ego to sickness, we should not ask the Holy Spirit to heal the body. Instead, we should ask Him to *teach us the proper perception of the body.* Only perception can be sick because only perception can be wrong.

The illusion of the body as self-reliant and able to overcome loneliness is part of the ego's plan to establish its own autonomy. When we believe being with another body is companionship, we are keeping our brother held in his body by guilt. We are looking on communication as dangerous. The ego teaches communication is the cause of loneliness and that loneliness is solved by guilt. Many have learned this foolish lesson. The Holy Spirit teaches communication is between minds. We will come into our true relationship with our brothers when we learn how to forgive each other.

All anger is an attempt to make another feel guilty. Anger is the ego's only basis for a relationship. The only need it has is for guilt. If we identify with the ego, then we will be attracted to guilt. To be with a body is not communication. If we believe it is, then we will be afraid to listen to the Holy Spirit.

Our challenge is to look at all the interference put up by the ego and recognize that what we think we want will not gratify us. We made the ego and the body as attempts to limit communication. Unlimited communication is the only means we have to establish real relationships. The body should be used to help us communicate with our brothers under the guidance of the Holy Spirit and to teach His message to all who are sent to us. When we follow His guidance we will be healed and so will our brothers.

Escape From Prison

A special relationship is an ego device for limiting ourselves to a body. It is used also to limit perception of others to their body. It is totally valueless without a body. If we value the special relationship, we must value the body.

The shadow figures that inhabit this world want us to believe the ego is holy. They teach us that what we do to keep it safe is really love. But they teach only vengeance, which they try to make us believe is love. Any relationship they enter into is totally insane. The purpose of these relationships is to exclude the truth about our brother and ourselves. That is why we see what is not there in both instead of the beauty. And that is why we are attracted to whatever reminds us of past grievances.

These relationships all become attempts at union through the body. Bodies are necessary before there can be an unholy relationship. Without a body we could not enter into a relationship in this world. Unholiness tries to reinforce itself, as does holiness, by surrounding itself with what it perceives as the same as itself.

In the unholy relationship the body, especially certain parts such as the face, is emphasized. It is used as the standard for comparison we make between our brothers. Reason will tell us this is an insane yardstick to use for measuring the worth of a brother. Let us learn to make no comparisons, we are all equal in God.

All minds are joined and bodies are not. Separation seems possible only when the mind is given the properties of the body by the ego. The ego convinces us we are a body. The mind seems to be splintered off by itself and alone. Its guilt is projected to the body, which suffers and dies. The mind can direct the body to act out fantasies. But the body never seems to satisfy the desires the mind has. The mind, frustrated, tries to attack the body by increasing the guilt it projects on it. The body attack is an attempt by the ego to keep separation in the mind and submerge the Identity of the mind.

It is insane to blame the body for what we wished it would do. The fantasies we wish for are impossible to act out. We still want them but they have nothing to do with what the body does. They make it a liability where it could be an asset. Fantasies have made our body our "enemy." It is weak, vulnerable and treacherous; worthy of our hate. We have identified with this thing we hate, a thing without meaning. We have proclaimed it to be the dwelling place of God's Son and turned it against him.

We made this host to God. Neither God nor His holy Son can enter a place that harbors hate. We made this thing to serve our guilt. It stands between us and other minds. We do not identify with them even though we are all joined. We see ourselves locked in a separate prison, incapable of reaching out or of being reached. We hate the prison and want to destroy it. But we do not want to escape from it without harming it, as long as our guilt is laid upon it. We still wish to remain in this world we made because we are afraid of leaving it for what is "unknown" to us.

The way we can escape is through the mind. The body is an illusion of ourselves. It limits the universal communication of our minds. The mind's communication is internal because the mind reaches only to itself. There is nothing outside the mind. We are entirely within it. It is entirely within us. There is nothing else, anywhere or ever. God's Kingdom of Heaven waits for us there.

The body seems to surround us and shut us off from others, but it is not really there. God cannot be separated from His Son and His Son cannot be separated from Him except in illusions. This could be the Son of God's reality only if God were wrong. He would have had to create differences to separate Himself from His Son and make this possible. He would have had to create different orders of reality, only some of which were love. But love is changeless, forever like itself and forever without alternatives. We cannot put a barrier around ourselves. God placed none between Himself and His Sons.

Everyone has experienced the feeling of being transported beyond himself – transcending time and place – or out of body. It is a sudden feeling of liberation from the body, a joining of something else in which our mind enlarges to encompass it. We unite with it as we become whole with it. The physical distance and what we join with makes no difference. It can occur with something in the past, present or future because time is not relevant. It can be a sound, a sight a thought or memory. We join it without reservation because we love it. Our limits melt away. The "laws" our body obeys are suspended.

In this escape the body is merely perceived properly. We have stopped being limited by it. We are not "lifted out" of it. It cannot contain us because that is not what we want. We are free to go where we want to, gaining a sense of Self. There is a lifting of the barriers of time and space, the sudden experience of peace and joy and the lack of awareness of the body. Questions on the feasibility of this experience are not asked. These experiences are similar to the holy instant, which will be covered in Chapter 6.

A Little Ship

We still put faith in the body as a source of strength. Every plan we make involves its comfort or protection or enjoyment in some way. The body is an end and not a means to us because we find sin attractive. We cannot accept the Atonement for ourselves if we still have sin as a goal.

The body is a limit on love. It was made to limit the unlimited – the Son of God. We identify external things by projecting them in a familiar form we can be comfortable with. We cannot even think of God without a body, or in a form we can recognize. With its tiny senses the body cannot have true knowledge. While we limit ourselves to it we will not see the grandeur surrounding us. Awareness of the body seems to make love limited. Trying to limit love, which is limitless, always will seem to shut God out and keep us isolated from Him.

The body is a fence around a tiny part of a grand and glorious idea. We proclaim our kingdom there, where God cannot enter. The ego is the cruel ruler in this kingdom. It calls on us to fight against the universe to defend this little speck of dust. Compared to the mind, this little fragment is like a tiny ship on a vast ocean. The ship arrogantly believes it is the ruler of the world it sees. But it fears the terrifying ocean. It believes the ocean wants to swallow it. However, the ocean continues serenely along, unaware of this frantic activity on a tiny point on its surface.

Those who believe they inhabit bodies in this world are like this little ship. Each body seems to be alone. It houses a separate mind, not connected to the Thought that created it. It appears to be self-sufficient. It needs another for some things, but it is not totally dependent on its one Creator for everything. It means nothing by itself for it has no life on its own.

The Self continues, unaware this tiny part regards itself as the only reality. But it could not exist by itself. The whole would not be whole without it. It is not a separate kingdom surrounded by a fence. It is not ruled by an idea that separates it from its Creator and the rest of the Sonship. Like the little ship, this little aspect is no different from the whole. It is not separate because its being was created as part of oneness.

The power that was given to us is far greater than in the ocean. We should not accept this isolated little part as ourselves. We should not strive to rule a tiny domain and be willing to die for defending it. Surrounding it with love is the glorious whole, offering it happiness and deep content. Love would never exclude the little self we set off by itself.

The Body is an Idol to the Ego

The world of bodies is made by an insane mind. The body's senses seem to prove the world we see is true. Our mind is constantly receiving insane messages from it via our senses. We do not receive any messages of what lies beneath all this. The messages are there but we have blocked them out. The body's eyes cannot perceive what is really there because the body's senses are completely unaware of it.

The body cannot be used for union. If we see a brother in a body we have set up a state in which union is impossible. Our faithlessness has separated us from each other. It keeps us both from being healed. We have opposed the Holy Spirit's purpose and illusions have come between us. We will perceive the body as seeming to be sick because we have made it the scapegoat of our guilt.

Truth and illusions are opposites. They cannot be perceived in the same place at the same time. If we try to seek both of these, we are setting an unobtainable goal. One of these is sought through the body, seeking reality through attack. The other seeks healing through the mind. To resolve this conflict the ego fosters the belief that the body must be healed, not the mind. This divided goal tries to give equal reality to both.

This is possible only if the mind is limited to the body and is divided into little, unconnected but seemingly whole parts. This cannot be, because all minds are joined as one. Healing is needed in the mind where the fantasy thought system is kept. The mind is sick, not the body, and that is where healing is needed. God gave healing where there is sickness by establishing the remedy in our minds – the Holy Spirit.

We believe the body is valuable for what it offers. This is an obstacle to our peace of mind. Guilt is attractive to those who think they dwell in a body. They prefer guilt to peace. The body is proof that guilt is real as long as they believe in it. Its actions are dictated by guilt. If we seek pleasure through the body, we will always find pain.

The body pursues guilt as the goal we set for it. The illusion of guilt is maintained by our attraction to it. The body seeks pain, because it obeys the idea pain is pleasure. This idea underlies the ego's whole investment in the body. It keeps this insane relationship hidden, but continues to feed on it. It teaches us the body's pleasure is our only happiness, but it tells itself, "Body pleasure leads to oblivion."

The body is like a communication medium. It has no feelings of its own. It receives and transmits messages to us about the feelings we believe we want. All of the feelings given to the messages are furnished by the sender and receiver. Both the ego and Holy Spirit know this. They also know the sender and receiver are the same entity. The Holy Spirit joyfully tells us this. The ego hides it. We would not send out messages of hatred and attack if we knew they were being sent back to us. We would not accuse, make guilty and condemn ourselves.

If we listen to this madness preached by the ego, we will believe the impossible is true. We should always remember the ego has dedicated the body to the goal of sin. Its followers sing the praises of the body, glorifying its reign. Every one of them must believe yielding to the attraction of guilt is the way to escape from pain. Every one of them must regard the body as his only self, without which he would die. But within it, his death is assured.

The body can only serve the purpose we give to it. It will be whatever we want to look on. If the body enters into a relationship, idolatry becomes the basis, not love. Love wants to be known, understood and shared. It has no secrets that it wants to keep from anyone. It walks sedately along, basking in the sunshine of honesty. It is sincere and smiles in welcome to all.

The ego uses the body as its weapon of choice to seek power through relationships. It wants unholy relationships solely for the offerings of idolatry it thrives on. Everything else is thrown away. It does not care about the other's feelings so long as it can be in control. It tries to place its idols in as many bodies as it can collect. They become its temples. Those who worship idols are afraid of love. Love is a threat to them because it ignores the body. When love approaches they flee in fear. What they fear is the beginning of their escape from prison.

The body is the ego's idol. It is the belief in sin projected outward, producing a wall of flesh around the mind. It seems to keep the mind prisoner in a tiny mite of space and time. It has only an instant to live and die. This unholy instant seems to be a life where the Son of God stops fleetingly to choose again between idol worship and love. He can choose between idolizing the body, or let himself be free of it.

The ego uses the body as the means to make an unholy relationship seem real. The purpose of the unholy relationship is sin. Sin can be attained only in illusions. A brother is seen as a body because that is the wish of those in the relationship and illusions always follow our wishes. The means is not questioned because the body's eyes adapt to the wish. The end is valued because sight always obeys the desire. The thought occurs first then we see what the thought projects. It we see the body then we have chosen judgement, not vision.

If we see a brother's body then we are judging him, not really seeing him. We imagine him in the darkness of sin where illusions are kept hidden from truth. We imagine his reality as a body in unholy relationships with other bodies. He is a slave to sin for an instant and then he dies.

The body can be looked on only through judgement. We see it because we lack vision. We have denied the means the Holy Spirit offers us to serve His purpose of training our mind to return to God. We taught ourselves judgement, but vision can be learned from Him. His vision cannot look on sin, so He cannot see the body. Our holy brother is no illusion. We should not try to see him in darkness. The body's eyes adjust to sin. They see it everywhere, in everything. Everything is seen as condemned when seen through them.

All those who see the body as everything anyone has, must adjust to where they live, afraid to lose the little they have. They keep failing to reach each other. They adjust to loneliness, believing the body is all they have.

A body demands the sacrifice of another body. The mind uses the body to carry out the means for sin in which the mind believes. Those who value sin believe in the joining of mind and body. Sacrifice is thus a means for limitation and therefor for hate. Hate leads to attack and attack keeps us separated from the Sonship and from our Father.

Let Us Use Our Reason

No one thinks only for himself, just as God does not think without His Son. This could be possible only if both were in bodies. A mind could think for itself only if the mind were part of the body. It is only bodies that can be separate, minds are always joined. Insanity is left by accepting reason where the madness was. Madness and reason see the same things but they look on them differently.

Reason does not attack. It replaces madness if the insane choose to listen to it. The insane do not know their will. They believe they see the body because their madness tells them it is real. Reason could not do that. If we try to defend the body against reason then we do not understand it or ourselves.

If we think our body separates us from our brother then we are insane. The body cannot be a barrier between what reason tells us must be joined. We could not see it if we listened to the voice of reason. Nothing can stand between what must be continuous.

Let reason take the next step. If we attack whom God wants healed and if we hate whom He loves, we must have a different will than our Creator. But if we are His Will, then we must believe we are not ourselves, we are somebody other than what God created. We have faith in this belief. Our senses show us evidence that we can see, hear and touch to support it. But we wonder where our strange uneasiness, our sense of being disconnected and our haunting fear of the lack of meaning in our lives comes from. It appears we have wandered into this life without any plan except to wander off again, in search of fulfillment.

These eyes were not made to see. The idea they represent did not leave its maker. The body's eyes are perfect means for not seeing. They stop at the nothingness of illusions, unable to go beyond the form to the meaning. The form binds our perception, obscuring our understanding. We peer blindly about in the darkness, thinking we are seeing when all we see are illusions.

God and the ego will never meet. We seem to meet the ego for our beliefs converge on the body. The body is the ego's chosen home and we believe it is ours also. So we meet at an error, the mistake in our self-appraisal. The ego joins us there with an illusion of ourselves. We share in the illusion but illusions cannot join. The ego, being nothing, cannot join with anything.

When we look in a mirror we will see a body. If we look at this body in a different light, it looks different. Without a light, we cannot see it so it appears to be gone. But we believe it is there because we can touch it with our hands and hear it move. It is an image of what we want to be in the dream world we think we are in. It is the means by which our dreams come true. It provides the eyes that we see it with, the hands we touch it with and the ears that hear the sounds it makes. The body proves its own reality to us.

The body is made as a theory of what we think we would like to be. But there are no provisions for evidence beyond what its five senses return and no escape from its fleshy prison is provided. We seem to be trapped in it without the key to escape. When seen through its eyes, its course is sure. It grows and withers, flourishes and dies. We cannot conceive of ourselves being something other than what it is. We hate its acts when it indulges itself, labeling it as sinful and judge it to be evil. But our specialness is very pleased with this "son" it spawned.

The "son" is now the means to serve his "father's" purpose. It is not like the "father" in any way. But it offers him what he wants. This is a travesty of God's creation. The creation of God's Son gave Him joy, returned His Love and shared His purpose. Similarly, the body testifies to the theory that made it.

When we see a brother in a body, separate from us, it is the expression of a wish to see only a little part of him, and sacrifice the rest. In this world we see nothing joined to anything beyond itself. Every living thing can come close together with other living things but can never really join.

The body is a loss of power, serenity and love. It can be made to sacrifice. When we see our brother as a body, we are demanding sacrifice of him and of ourselves. The greatest sacrifice demanded is that God's Son see himself without his Father and his Father be without His Son. Every sacrifice demands they be separate. If any sacrifice is asked of anyone, the memory of God will be denied. God's Son is invisible in a world of separate bodies. His song of love and unity cannot be heard. But he can make the world recede before his song.

The body has no purpose by itself. It holds all our memories and hopes. We use its eyes to see, ears to hear and let it tell us what it feels; but it does not hold any knowledge. It tells us only the names we gave it to use when we call upon the players in the script we wrote. These shadow figures in our dreams seem to prove its reality. We can choose among the names given to the body but they are all the same.

The body is the central figure in the dreaming of the world. Every dream holds a body that acts as if it were a person to be seen and believed. Every dream tells how it was made by other bodies by being born into the world outside the body. It lives a while then dies, to be united in the dust with other bodies that also died. It seeks for other bodies to be its friends and/or enemies in the brief time allotted to it. Its main concerns are its safety and comfort. It looks for pleasure and tries to avoid what would harm it. Most important, it tries to teach itself that its pains and joys are different, and can be told apart.

The dreaming of the world takes many forms. The body seems to prove it is autonomous and real in many ways. It works to get money, doing senseless things. It wastes the money on senseless things it does not need and does not even want. It puts things on itself that it has bought to protect itself and/or make itself attractive to another body. It hires other bodies to protect it. It looks about for special bodies to share its dream. Sometimes it dreams it is a conqueror of other bodies weaker than itself. Sometimes it dreams it is the slave of bodies that would hurt it. It shares its illusions with other dreamers who agree with its assessment of itself.

But it is the body that is the prisoner. The body does not think or learn. It holds the willing mind in a prison. It becomes sick at the bidding of the mind. It grows old, withers and dies at the bidding of the mind because the mind is sick. The only thing that can cause change is learning – and the mind *can* learn. All change is made there.

"Never fear shadows. They simply mean there is a light shining somewhere nearby."

Ruth Renkel

Chapter 5

OVERCOMING FEAR

Introduction

Their are only two emotions – love and fear. When we feel fear, it is simply an absence of perfect love. With God, only perfect love exists, and, since we are part of God, fear is an impossible state. If we feel fearful, then we do not have perfect love. Since only perfect love exists, if there is fear then the result is a state that does not exist.

Whenever a fearful situation arises, the fear can be removed by consciously repeating, "I choose love instead of fear." All fear is based on the subconscious thought we are more powerful than God and so it is really a fear of God because we are afraid of retaliation by God.

We are afraid of being released from the prison we made because we do not know what the alternative is and we fear the unknown. We believe that any harm can be confined solely to the body. But we have a subconscious fear that the mind can hurt itself. These errors can be corrected by remembering that only the mind can create and it is our mistaken thoughts that need correction.

The Beginning of Healing

Miracles are a means of abolishing fear. A miracle leads to revelation, a state in which there is no fear. Forgiveness replaces the emptiness caused by fear. All healing is a release from fear and is the result of miracles. The Atonement, the final miracle, is the remedy for all errors. To begin our healing, it is important that we learn to let go of our fear because it will interfere with our understanding of the Atonement principle. We should learn to accept the Atonement and place It at the center of our inner altar. It is the perfect defense against all separation and fear thoughts.

We believe that what we made is true because our senses report back to us what we sent them out to find. We made fear and we believe we can never control its effects ourselves. The purpose of the world is to correct wrong beliefs such as this one.

When we accept the Atonement we will escape from fear because we will realize that our errors never occurred. This can be compared to what happens during a nightmare when an external bright light is seen as part of the dream and therefor seems to be fearful. But upon awakening, the light is seen as freeing us from the dream, which we then recognize as being an illusion. In reality, this light is knowledge and as we learn, it will grow brighter in our sight.

Exposure to a miracle may increase our fear until we become panicky. In these cases, a compromise between mind and body, something material (i.e. medicine) to alleviate the fear can be used. Magic is the creative process of the mind gone wrong. The medications that we use are "spells." But we should continue to use them as long as we are fearful of the mind's healing process. We are fearful because we do not recognize the Source of healing. This fear makes us feel vulnerable so we become even more fearful. Under these circumstances we should not attempt to perform miracles.

To perform a miracle of healing we should put perfect trust in our elder brother's readiness to perform them. When we try to rely on our own readiness, fear will enter. Or, as with all forms of fear, we have not accepted the Atonement for ourselves.

To be a miracle worker we must accept the Atonement for ourselves. This is our sole responsibility. We can give the healing message of the Atonement to others and teach them that the illusions they made cannot hurt them. When this lesson is learned we will stop thinking of the body as the learner and restore the mind to this function.

The body is a learning device, the mind is the learner. The body can be an obstacle to learning if we attach any significance to it. The mind can be filled with light and can bring the body into alignment with itself when it realizes it is the learner, not the body. When this happens we will be on the road to peace. The way to start is to be happy and offer kindness and mercy to everyone. The Holy Spirit wants us to always be happy. We will discover one of the basic laws of God in operation. Whatever we give to our brothers we give to ourselves. When we make them happy, we are making ourselves happy at the same time.

Our elder brother's guidance can direct everything that is important. He also can take control of everything that is not important, but our fear prevents him. He cannot control our fear, only we can do that. Fear is merely body thoughts that we have raised to the level of the mind because we feel responsible for them.

We must change our mind to have healing. We must be *willing* to let our mind be guided so correction can occur at the right level. When the mind is healed then our behavior will be corrected.

To overcome our fear we should ask for help in the circumstances that caused it. The wish to be separate is always involved in some way in causing fear. We can correct this wish. Before we choose to do anything we should ask our elder brother if it is in accordance with his choice.

Fear results when what we do is in conflict with our will. There are two ways this can happen: a) We choose to do conflicting things. In this case, the part of the mind that wants to do something else is outraged. b) We do what we think we should - but without fully wanting to. In this case we are being consistent but we are under great strain.

In both these cases we are doing something we do not wholly want to do. This produces rage and we usually project it onto the world we see. Correcting our behavior just shifts the error from a) to b), but the fear remains. It is our thinking that needs correction.

The mind can be brought under our elder brother's guidance automatically when we become *willing* to do God's Will. This decision must be made without any reservations. Then we will stop being in conflict with what our will wants us to do. With the conflict gone, the mind will stop producing fear.

When a conflict arises there are steps that can be taken to correct the situation. The first corrective step is to know that the result of the conflict is an expression of fear. Second, realize that fear arises from a lack of love. Third, the only remedy for a lack of love is perfect love. Fourth, know that perfect love is the Atonement. These steps in undoing the error are part of the larger process of accepting the Atonement.

The expression of the Atonement – the miracle – is always an expression of respect between equally worthy brothers. When we are afraid it is because we have chosen to do something without love. This is the need the Atonement was established to fill. When we accept the Atonement the fear will be gone, which is true healing.

We persist in making ourselves fearful even though fear does not exist. Our elder brother cannot intervene between our thoughts and their results as this would be tampering with a basic law of cause and effect. It would not be helpful if he belittled the power of our thinking. We are all equal in sharing the Mind of God. Instead, we have to learn to guard our thoughts more carefully. We need to learn miracle-minded thinking.

Miracle Minded Thinking

We can choose either fear or the miracle. Both come from our thoughts and we can control them. In the past we have been afraid of everything and everyone. We are afraid of God, of our elder brother and of ourselves. We have perceived all of them incorrectly. Consequently we have made them incorrectly and we believe in what we have made. We did this because we are afraid of our thoughts, and being afraid has caused us pain. We fear God because we have used our minds to miscreate.

This is the fundamental conflict in this world, creation versus miscreation. All love is implicit in creation and all fear is implicit in miscreation. The conflict, then, is always between love and fear. The only way we can master fear is through love. Fear, which is nothing, cannot coexist with love, which is everything. A compromise between everything and nothing is impossible. We have chosen to fear love because of its perfect harmlessness.

We are constantly judging ourselves and our brothers. This creates an intolerable strain that saps our energy. We are in no position to judge, since we do not have the knowledge. But we cherish our ability to judge because we want to be the author of our own reality; we want to be in control. This causes us to be fearful of judgement on ourselves since we use it as a weapon in our defense of our own authority. What we should do when the need for judgement rises, is let the Holy Spirit make all judgements, that is His function. Fear rises from our attempt to judge what lies far beyond our ability to judge. We should not try to judge but ask Him and then wait patiently for the Holy Spirit's judgment.

As we approach the Beginning, we will find our Self still in peace. But we are afraid to go back because we believe our thought system – what we think of as ourselves – will be destroyed. This is really a fear of death, but there is no death, only a belief in death. When we fear salvation, we are choosing the death, darkness and perception of this world instead of the life, light and knowledge of the real world.

Fear and love cannot coexist. It is impossible to be wholly fearful and remain alive. Therefor, the only possible whole state is that of love. Since love and joy are the same, the only possible whole state is wholly joyous, which is healing.

To heal is to make happy and it does not matter to what part or by what part healing is made, the whole Sonship benefits equally. To be healed is to accept the Atonement.

The Holy Spirit is part of our brother's mind as well as part of ours. When we share the Voice of the Holy Spirit It becomes stronger in us. Our lack of willingness to hear It and our fondness for grievances has made It weak in our mind. When we look for It in ourselves alone we are embarking on an ego trip, which will produce only fear.

The Holy Spirit will help us out of fear by showing us everything we perceive as fearful is just a lack of love. By joining the Atonement we will escape our fears. Only what is loving is true. Nothing that is good can be lost and nothing that is not good can be protected. The ego fades away when we hear the Holy Spirit's call to be one with our brothers. We cannot cancel out our past errors alone, we need our brother's love and forgiveness.

If we identify with the ego, we will experience guilt and be fearful of punishment. The ego is always wrong because its decisions are based on judgement. The Holy Spirit always reverses the ego's decisions. When time comes to an end the ego will not be destroyed. It will be reinterpreted and the part of our mind we gave to the ego will be returned to the Kingdom. This will release us from fear.

Produced by fear, the ego reproduces fear. The ego does not love us, but love is our power, which the ego denies. Love is everything and gives us everything. The ego's purpose is fear and it makes us fearful. Only the fearful can be egotistical. We are fearful because we believe a brother is attacking us to tear the Kingdom of Heaven from us.

When we avoid the Holy Spirit's guidance it is because we want to be fearful. Our elder brother will deny us nothing on our journey back to God. When fear intrudes, it is the ego trying to join the journey. It cannot and becomes angry and spiteful. When we fly into a rage for what we later realize is a silly reason, it is because we have been listening to the ego's guidance instead of to the Holy Spirit's.

All healing involves replacing fear with love. Healing is replacing the fear of waking with the decision to wake. Certain specific forms of healing are not achieved (i.e. not what we think we want) even when the state of healing is. We may ask for healing of a specific physical ailment. If we were healed, the threat to our thought system may be far more fearful to us than its physical expression. We are not asking for release from fear but removal of a symptom we have chosen.

In our dream state we are denying reality. We have accepted something else in its place. This is always fearful because it is an attack on truth and truth is God. When we attack we are denying ourselves. We always attack ourselves first because we are part of God, as is the person we think we are attacking.

Happiness will come only when what we do is in accordance with our will. Sickness happens because we are afraid to know God's Will. Every fear and every sickness arises from our belief God's Will is not our will. We want what it *is not* our will to have and do not want what it *is* our will to have. We hide in darkness because we do not want to know our will is in accordance with God's Will.

Fear is a Call for Love

The journey we travel in this world follows the way of pain, fear and grief. This dark journey is not the province of God's Son. Let us instead walk in the light of our Father's Kingdom. We should not fear the illusions we made, for what is nothing cannot be fearful. The way is not hard, but it *is* very different. The Great Light always surrounds us and shines out from us so our brothers can see the way with us and we can see the way with them. We cannot see the shadow figures in the light. If we deny them instead of denying the light, the way will be clear.

Healing is the removal of all that stands in the way of knowledge. We should not be afraid to look at illusions because we will be looking at the source of fear and fear is not real. Its effects can be dispelled merely by denying they exist. If there are no effects, then fear does not exist. If we look closely at fear then we will realize it cannot be seen.

The ego does not want us to realize we are afraid of it. If it caused us to be fearful, our independence would be reduced and our power weakened. We ally ourselves with the ego because we believe it can give us power and keep us independent. Its existence could not continue if we realized we were belittling ourselves and depriving ourselves of power by following its dictates.

The basic teaching of the ego is the fear of God. When we recognize that fear is all that seems to separate us from God, the ego is shaken to the foundation of its dream of autonomy. We will not accept the cost of fear once we recognize it. When we ignore love we are denying ourselves. We think that we have successfully attacked truth. We are afraid of ourselves because we think that our thoughts would destroy us.

We are always pursuing the ego's goal of autonomy. Our personal independence or separation from our brothers is very precious to the ego-thinking part of our mind. If we let ourselves be guided by the ego we maintain a space – a defense zone – between ourselves and our brothers. But it has brought us only fear despite the ego's belief that it will bring safety and happiness.

We are afraid of the world we see. What we think we see is a world of taking, getting and spending. We have lost sight of the real world; but it is still ours for the asking. If we ask for the truth of God without fear, His answer will release us from fear.

If we use the Holy Spirit's criteria to recognize fear, we will become aware of the need for escape from fear. We can let the Holy Spirit change the fear into truth by facing the fear without trying to disguise it. We should use His interpretation of the motives of others, not our own. Let us accept only their loving thoughts and look at all else as an appeal for help. Attack is a call for love. Only attack produces fear. Let us recognize fear for what it really is – a call for love.

Fear's purpose is to conceal love. We are capable of only two emotions; fear and love. Fear stems from our own deep sense of loss because of our separation from the Sonship and from our Father. By easing the loss in others – by the wish to join with our brothers – we can remove the basic cause of fear in ourselves. Fear is a false emotion, being made out of denial. If we realize fear is a mask for the underlying belief in love then fear is made useless and will be discarded.

The reality of the world is love. We can learn its reality by answering every appeal for love by giving it instead of answering attack with attack. The gift we give our brothers is the gift we give ourselves. We can learn from the Holy Spirit how to replace fear with love by asking Him. Then we can learn how to replace our dream of separation and accept the unity of the Sonship.

If we choose to rid ourselves of fear, we will succeed because God always is with us. When fear is overcome we become aware that He lives in us. We can do this by not denying fear's full effect in any way. Let us look forthrightly at our fears and let the Holy Spirit judge any situation truly. His light will shine our fears away if we will only offer them to Him.

If we exclude one brother from our love, we hide a secret place in our mind where the Holy Spirit is not welcome. We will not be completely healed until we offer total love for all the Sonship. Even one small spot of fear will exclude healing. Love cannot enter where there is any fear.

Keep no Secrets From the Holy Spirit

Fear has many forms. Each individual makes his own private world with his own insane forms of fear. He alone perceives the sights and sounds of his private world. In our private world we react to love as if it were fear, and to fear as if it were love. We are drawn to fear and populate our world with figures of fear. Love repels us so we do not see all the love our brothers offer us.

The only way to look within and see the light of love is to release our brothers from guilt as we want to be released. We who have always loved the Father can not be afraid to look within because love is guiltless. The Holy Spirit will restore reason to us by removing all illusions. Reason will tell us that our guilt is not reasonable. It is not in the Mind of God where we are. The Holy Spirit will show us the perfect purity shining in us through Christ's vision.

The hidden cannot be shared so it cannot be loved. What cannot be loved must be feared. The Holy Spirit lives within us in the light of perfect openness. Nothing is hidden so nothing is fearful to Him. The light of love will dispel all darkness except what has been kept secret from love.

Truth is always there, within us. It becomes unreal to us if we hide it by surrounding it with fear. To find it, we have to honestly search out everything interfering with it. It is hidden beneath the cornerstones of fear which are part of the ego's insane belief system that we erected. Let us look honestly at fear and it will fade away as truth emerges from it.

Here is all the Holy Spirit asks of us:

- Bring every secret we have locked away to Him.
- Open every door in our mind to Him.
- Invite Him into the darkness to shine it away.
- Look with Him or He cannot see what we hide.
- Bring all our dark and secret thoughts to Him and look upon them with Him.

He will enter gladly and shine away our fears. But if we hide anything from Him, He cannot look upon it. The vision of Christ is for Him and for us. When we both look upon the light He holds and the darkness we hold, they cannot coexist. If we join our perception to His, then His judgement will triumph.

Every problem we have can be solved by a miracle the Holy Spirit will offer to us. Every trial or fear or pain has been brought to light by Him and undone. Miracles are not for a select few, they are for everyone. He has shone His Light on all our dark lessons, recognizing they never had any existence in reality. Lessons we want to teach ourselves do not exist in His mind. He has corrected them. We have taught ourselves wrongly in the past. But He does not see the past. His lessons are the only ones we should use for our re-education.

In this world we are afraid of death because we are not aware there is no death. The ego's goal is hell, teaching us that hell is in our future. It does not believe in what it teaches – death and dissolution. If we thought of death as an end to pain, would we fear it? This is typical of the ego's thought system. It seems to protect us from fear so it can keep us as an ally. But it needs to produce fear to maintain itself. It cannot conceive of its own death so it teaches death ends the hope of Heaven

The only hell is what the ego has made of the present. We do not understand the present because of our belief in and fear of hell. The Holy Spirit uses the present to undo the fear by which the ego would make the present useless. In the ego's use of time fear is inescapable. The ego teaches time is a teaching device to compound guilt. Guilt becomes so all-encompassing that vengeance is always demanded.

The Holy Spirit teaches fear can only be in the past or future which do not exist in the present *now*. Every miracle He offers us corrects our use of time. When each instant stands by itself, clear of the past and without its shadow reaching into the future, fear will be gone. The Son of God will emerge from the past into each clean instant in the present. Each instant is an untarnished birth extending the present forever. There is only happiness, free of guilt in the present *now*. Darkness is forgotten and immortality and joy are there in the *now*.

Guilt causes fear. Only perfect love has no fear. Special relationships frequently shift and change because they have some fear in them. We have chosen our special relationships to support the ego. The Holy Spirit will use them as learning experiences to become lessons in love for us. Under His guidance, our relationship can teach us the power of love, making all fear impossible.

This will be explained in Chapter 7

Sacrifice is Not Love

Fear takes many forms. If we examine them as different symptoms of an idea that we do not want, then they become one concept. The idea is this: we believe we can choose to be host to God or hostage to the ego. We think we must make this decision because we believe sacrifice is essential to love. Sacrifice is a fundamental part of our thought system. If there is sacrifice, someone must pay and someone must get. Salvation apart from sacrifice means nothing to us. But sacrifice is attack, not love. If we accept this idea, our fear of love will vanish and our guilt will disappear.

To sacrifice something for another is not love. Sacrifice always brings guilt and love always brings peace. We exclude our brothers and our Father through guilt. When we exclude someone they become fearful to us. Love invites them back. We try to cast out part of ourselves and provide it with a fearful nature. We cannot have peace if we perceive part of ourselves as loathsome for we will experience ourselves as incomplete and lonely.

Every illusion is one of fear. If we try to escape from one to the other we will fail. We seek love outside ourselves because we sense there is hatred within ourselves. Peace will not come from the illusion of love.

Those who choose certain partners to live with and use them for purposes they would not share with others, are trying to live with guilt rather than die of it. They see love as an escape from death, and seek it desperately. It would gladly come quietly if they sought it in peace. When they still fear death, the relationship loses the illusion of love. Fear rushes in then and the hatred triumphs.

Love calls us on a journey but hate calls us to stay. We should not see any fantasies nor heed hate's call. They are our calls for help, endlessly rising from us to our Creator. He answers us because He loves us, wholly without illusion. Love is wholly without illusion, therefor wholly without fear. In His link with us, God has never forgotten us, who make Him whole. In His link with us is our ability to remember His Wholeness and His gratitude to us for His completion.

In an unholy relationship the other seems to possess a special self. He is "loved" for this "better" self. But it can be taken away at any time. If both partners see this special self, this is the ego's "perfect union, made in Heaven." This illusion of Heaven is really an attractive form of fear. It is offered by the ego to interfere with Heaven. The guilt is buried deep, rising in the form of "love."

When the light comes nearer in our dream, we rush off to the darkness, retreating in fear. We shrink from the truth. But we can advance when we change our goal so that it becomes moving from fear to truth. If we show that we are willing to accept the goal of knowledge, we can join with our elder brother in an instant of light. When we have stepped back in fear into the darkness he will remind us that our goal is the light. All the means by which salvation is achieved are only aspects of the plan to change our dreams of fear to happy dreams, from which we wake to knowledge.

The holy instant will remove all fear and hatred from our mind. We should never try to remove them ourselves because that is its function. We should not try to overlook our guilt before we ask the Holy Spirit for help. That is His function. We should offer Him a little *willingness* to let Him remove all fear and hatred and to be forgiven. That is all. He will take our little faith, join it with His understanding, and build our part in the Atonement. The holy instant will be explained in Chapter 7.

The whole world seems to be based on the circle of fear. It lies just below the level the body's eyes see. All the illusions, twisted thoughts, insane attacks, fury, vengeance, lust, greed and betrayal are here. They were made to keep the guilt in place, so the world could rise from it and keep it hidden. Guilt's shadow rises to the surface, just beneath our conscious thoughts. But its intensity is veiled by heavy coverings put there by the ego.

Love can never look on guilt. The attraction of guilt produces a fear of love. Love only looks on truth, seeing itself, with which it wants to unite in holy union. Fear cannot see love and so interferes with it. Love looks past fear and embraces the end of all guilt. Love never attacks so could never be afraid. Fear is attracted to what love does not see. Each believes that what the other looks upon does not exist. Fear looks with devotion on guilt, just as love looks on itself. Each sends out messengers which return messages that are a mirror of the language they were sent out with.

The Holy Spirit's Messengers

We are constantly sending out our messengers into the world to return with the messages we want. Love's messengers are gently sent. They return with messages of love and gentleness. Fear's messengers are ordered to seek out every scrap of guilt, sin and evil they can find. Love cannot even see what fear demands. Guilt's attraction is absent from love's gentle perception. What love looks on is meaningless to fear.

Relationships in this world depend on which emotion is used when we send the messengers out. Fear's messengers sneak off in search of guilt. Fear is merciless, even to its friends. But if we send the Holy Spirit's messengers we will not see fear any more. The only fear in this world is what we put there. It will be transformed, cleansed of all guilt and made beautiful when the Holy Spirit's messengers are sent.

We think giving ourselves over to peace would rob us of the body, leaving us homeless. We do not want to make this "sacrifice". But the body has never really given us anything. It does not justify our strange belief that in it lies salvation. Belief in the body is the belief in death. The body is the focus of the idea of atonement as murder. It is the source of the idea love is fear. All our thoughts in the thinking of this world in some way involve the body. It sends a constant stream of signals to the brain that assure its existence. We are always aware of its comfort or lack thereof, of its pain or pleasure, of its visual appeal, and of its appetites.

The Fear of Death

The unholy, or special, relationship is fundamental to our understanding. The ego sees it as proof of sin. But it is not punishment. It is the result of equating ourselves with a body. This invites pain because fear has been invited in, becoming our purpose. The attraction of guilt always enters with fear. What fear directs the body to do is always painful. The illusion of pleasure will also be experienced, sharing in the pain. We will confuse the pain with pleasure.

Death is made by the ego. The specter of its dark shadow falls over all living things. The fear of death is really its attraction, just as guilt is feared and is fearful. In our dream state we get a thrill out of fear. But guilt has no hold except on those who seek it out. It is the same with death. No one can die unless he chooses death.

Our seeming love for death is an obstacle to our peace. In it are all the ego's secrets. Here is the final end of union, the triumph of lifelessness over Life itself. But the fear of death will yield to the attraction of love. Without the fear of death we would remember our Father. When the fear of death is gone the light behind the veil will burn the veil away and our vision will no longer be clouded. We will find that when we overcome our fear of love, the whole world will suddenly look beautiful and bright to us, filled with joy. We will wonder why we stayed in the darkness for so long when it is so easy to emerge into the light.

The Holy Spirit will remain with us and when we raise our eyes we will be ready to look on terror without fear. We can look on the fear of God only when we have accepted the Atonement.

Some preparation is needed before we can look upon the fear of God. The sane can look on insanity with pity but not with fear. And as long as we share in insanity, it does seem fearful. We share in it until we can look on our brother with perfect faith and love and tenderness. We still are unforgiving in our insanity and we are afraid of those we do not forgive. We are afraid of God because we are afraid of our brother. No one can reach out to love with fear beside him.

We do not know our brother who stands beside us. He still seems to be a stranger. We want to keep what we think of as ourselves unharmed so we attack him, thinking he is fearful. But our salvation is in his hands. We hate his madness because we share in it. Instead of the pity and forgiveness that would heal it, we are afraid. We need to forgive each other for we will share in madness or Heaven together. We need each other, we will raise our eyes in faith together or not at all. When we do, we will no longer fear God.

This world is a judgement on ourselves. It is not really there, we have invented it. But judgement justifies it, making

---

"O, that this too too solid flesh would melt,
Thaw and resolve itself into a dew!
Or that the Everlasting had not fix'd
His canon 'gainst self-slaughter! O God! God!
How weary, stale, flat, and unprofitable
Seem to me all the uses of this world!"
William Shakespeare: Hamlet

it seem real. This sick picture is an image made by the ego, which carefully preserves it. The ego loves it and places it outside us where we adjust to living in its world. It is a merciless world. If it really was the outside world, we should be afraid. But since we made it, it can be corrected.

Those who desire to look upon their brothers in holiness and free them from the body can have no fear. They chose to let all false limits be removed. They chose to recognize how much their faith in the ego's world had limited their understanding. They desired to place the power of their faith somewhere else. All who choose to look away from sin will be given vision. Sin is a limit and whom we limit to a body, we hate because we fear them. What we fear within our brother is what makes God fearful to us.

The ego smiles in approval at fear in connection with sin. It does not doubt our belief and faith in sin because this proves our desire to have sin. But sin is impossible. If sin were so, then it would apply equally to the whole Sonship. And what is true for the Sonship is also true for God. Everyone knows sin is impossible for God. We should not let our fear of sin protect it from correction.

The ego tells us not to look inward. It tells us we would see sin and God would strike us blind. The ego has its own hidden fear about looking within, because it is not certain what would happen. There is another fear the ego has beneath the fear to look within.

What if we looked there and saw no sin? If we ask this question, we threaten the ego's whole defense system its very basis for existing. It can no longer pretend to be our friend. Those who have joined in a holy relationship, which will be described in Chapter 7, no longer believe their identity lies in the ego.

Guilt is attractive because of the fear it brings. Fear is the one emotion we made, the emotion of secrecy, of private thoughts and of the body. It opposes love. It leads to belief in differences and the loss of sameness. It keeps us blind, dependent on the self we think we made to lead us through the world fear made for us.

Miracles Will Overcome Fear

Conflict is always between two opposing forces. It cannot exist between one with power and one with nothingness. Anything we attack is part of ourselves. By attacking it we make two illusions of ourselves, in conflict with each other. This happens whenever we look on anything that God created with *anything* but love. Conflict is the birth of fear. When conflict causes strife, the strife does not make the conflict a part of reality.

We have filled our world with conflicts with ourselves. It is a world that seems to be in constant turmoil because of all the strife. But if we let it all be undone for us, then we will find the peace we are seeking. The way to do this is to turn to the remembrance of God, which is in our mind. God is the only place of safety in a world filled with illusions in conflict. The fear of Him is the fear of life, not of death.

Illusions make us fearful because of the beliefs they imply, not for the forms they take. The sole intent of attack is murder. The murderer must feel guilt and be fearful of punishment. When we attack a brother, we feel the fear of punishment. What is not love is murder. What is not loving is an attack. Any of the negative emotions, fear, envy, malice, greed, lust, jealousy, anger, etc. are really alternate forms of attack.

The Son of God invented an unholy relationship between himself and his Father so he could be free to play childish games of war. It is a fragmented relationship which limits the power of the Son of God. It is full of fear and leads to the destruction of the self. The world we perceive with the body's eyes fills us with fear. We think we can find some peace and satisfaction in it. But, despite our hopes, despair is always the result. There never is and never will be an exception to this. The only lesson from the past is – it gave us no rewards we want to keep. If we honestly look at the past, we should be willing to let it go forever. We have never been rewarded with anything but fear and guilt

The Son of God asks far too little here by believing he is limited by the body he made. To find a little treasure of his own, he wants to sacrifice his own Identity, which was given everything by God. He cannot do this without a sense of isolation, loss and loneliness. He can only be afraid of this treasure he calls his own. But fear is not treasure. We do not want uncertainty. It is merely a mistake about our will and what we really are, and, as such, can be corrected..

When good health is demonstrated, it is proved. If we wish only to be healed, we will heal. Our single purpose of mind makes this possible. If we are afraid of healing, we cannot be the agents of healing by coupling belief with faith. Our lack of fear is all that is required. The fearful cannot be healed, and cannot heal. This does not mean the conflict has to be gone forever from our mind to heal. It means that, only for an instant, we love without attack. All that is needed is an instant. Miracles do not wait on time. A miracle is *now*. It is already here. It exists in the only interval of time sin and fear have overlooked, but which is all there is to time. If we shrink from giving our blessing to anyone, the world will seem to be fearful.

Our suffering, by whatever name we called it, will be gone. The Holy Spirit perceives them all as one, and He calls them all fear. Fear is the champion of death and the miracle is the champion of life.

Waking From the Dream

Accepting the Atonement for ourselves, as described in Chapter 9, means not giving support to someone's dream of sickness and death. It means we do not share his wish to separate and turn his illusions on himself. Nor do we wish they be turned on us. Then they can have no effects on us. Unless we help him, we will suffer pain with him because that is our wish. We become a figure in his dream of pain as he does in ours. We both become illusions, without identity. Depending on whose evil dream we share, we could be anybody or anything. But it is certain we are evil, for we share in dreams of fear.

We think we are in a dream and we are afraid of it. God is the Alternate to dreams of fear. If we share in them, we can never share in Him. But if we withdraw our mind from sharing the evil dreams, then we share Him. There is no other choice. It is God's Will that we complete Himself.

The fear of God underlies our dreams of fear. The fear of God is the greatest obstacle to peace. We should never say we are God-fearing Christians (or some other religious denomination.) We should learn to say we are God-loving. Love seems to be treacherous to those who are afraid. Where there is fear, hate soon follows. He who hates is afraid of love, so he must be afraid of God. He does not know what love means. He fears to love and loves to hate. He thinks love is fearful and hate is love. This is what the little gap between brothers does to those who cherish it and think it is their salvation.

There are some dreams we think we like. But they hold us back as much as those with fear in them. Every dream is really a dream of fear, no matter what form it takes. All dreams hold the theme of depression or assault because they are made of fear. They may be disguised as pleasure but really have fear at their core The miracle allows us to lose our fear. It prepares the way for us to wake up.

When we give our dreams to the Holy Spirit He accepts them and uses them as a means to wake us. He changes our dreams of fear to happy dreams. He transforms any special relationship so it becomes a source of joy and freedom, with the guilt and pain gone. Its holiness will become an offering of blessing to everyone.

We are fearful whenever we do not feel a deep content, or are certain we are being helped, or we have a calm assurance that Heaven is with us. When we feel fear in any form, we have made an idol and believe it will betray us. Beneath our hope the idol will save us is the guilty feeling that we have betrayed ourselves.

Forgiving dreams remind us that we have not attacked ourselves and we live in safety. Our childish fears will disappear when we forgive ourselves. Dreams will become a sign we have made a new beginning. Forgiving dreams are kind to everyone who figures in the dream. They release the dreamer from fear. The dreamer has judged no one so he does not fear judgement. He remembers what he forgot when judgement seemed to be the way to save him from its penalty.

Choose Heaven or Hell

Let us look once more on our enemy, the one we chose to hate instead of love, the one who is standing here beside us. For that is how hatred was born into the world and the rule of fear established. Hate is the father of fear. Instead, let us hear God speak to us through Him Who is His Voice and ours as well. He will remind us it is not our will to hate, be a prisoner of fear, a slave to death or a little creature with a little life.

We should not be fooled by appearances. They only deceive and obscure reality and reflect our inner thoughts projected outwards. They bring fear because they hide the truth. If we attack what we made to deceive ourselves, we only prove we have been deceived.

The fear of God results from seeing pardon as being unearned. All who see themselves as guilty must fear God. God would be fearful if His Son, whom He created innocent, could be a slave to guilt. In guilt, God's perfect Son has forgotten

---

"The glory of friendship is not in the outstretched hand, nor in the kindly smile, nor the joy of companionship; it is in the spiritual inspiration that comes to one when he discovers that someone else believes in him and is willing to trust him."

Ralph Waldo Emerson

what he really is. The lesson that God's Son is guilty results in the fear of God.

The concept of the self stands between us and the truth. We only see images that we have made. We look on them through a barrier that dims our vision. The light is kept from everything we see. We look on imaginings that come from concepts born of fear. What we see is hell because fear is hell. But we have been given the vision and the inner Guide that will lead us out of hell with our loved ones beside us.

We must be vigilant against temptation. Let us remember it is only an insane wish to make ourselves into a thing we are not. It is a thing of madness, pain and death; of treachery and despair, with no hope except to die and end the dream of fear. *This* is temptation. Could it be difficult to choose against this? There are only two real alternatives we can choose between. We can choose only between Heaven or hell.

Giving up the separation not only gets rid of our fears but also brings the joy, peace and glory of creation to us. Let us offer the Holy Spirit only our *willingness* to remember God and return to Him so we will no longer be separate. He will tell us that we are part of God. God is in our memory and in this remembering is the knowledge of ourselves. Let us gladly give up everything in this world that would delay our remembrance of Him.

"There is no fear in love. But perfect love drives out fear, because fear has to do with punishment. The one who fears is not made perfect in love."

John 4:18

Chapter 6

THE REAL WORLD THROUGH FORGIVENESS

Introduction

In this dream world of shadow figures we believe we have sinned against our brothers. The resulting guilt has caused us all our woe. We can find our way out of this predicament only through complete forgiveness. By forgiving ourselves and our brothers we will fulfill the function given to us by God and find our true happiness. Forgiveness offers nothing less than the salvation of this world we have made. When our forgiveness is complete we will be in a position to accept the Atonement and our physical sight will be changed to the vision of Christ.

> **Forgiveness** - is a selective remembering of love thoughts and acts we gave to ourselves or to others in the past. It is remembering only the love thoughts and acts that were given to us in the past. It replaces the emptiness generated by fear. It heals the perception of separation. It is the forgetting of all the grievances we held against our brothers in the past. It is the wish to join with our brother.

Forgiveness can free the mind from believing the body is its home and restore the peace that God intended us to have. Forgiveness is the means by which we can overcome the fear of death.

Forgiveness means to forgive all the illusions we held against our brothers. We can release them from the slavery of their illusions by forgiving them for the illusions we perceive in them.

We can find peace only when we want to learn about complete forgiveness from the Holy Spirit. We made a world where we think we lack things. Before the separation we had everything. We believe we have deprived ourselves by setting up a set of false needs. These needs were established by our self-concept – the ego.

Learning About Forgiveness

Forgiveness has to be learned. The Holy Spirit will teach us all about forgiveness if we just ask Him. Through miracles we accept God's forgiveness and His Love. And we give only love, or forgiveness, to all living things. The miracle adjusts the mind to the right-minded, or spirit, level where we can understand healing. If forgiveness does not come from our right-mindedness it will not heal because it is judgmental. Miracle-minded forgiveness corrects our thoughts without evaluating (i.e. judging) the person we are forgiving. "Father forgive them for they know not what they do." makes no judgement but is an appeal to God to heal their minds.

The only meaningful prayer is for forgiveness, being a request that we recognize that we already have everything. We have lost the knowledge that we are a miracle of God. When we pray we should not ask God to forgive us. We should ask Him to teach us how to forgive.

The ego's plan of forgiveness is to see error clearly first and then overlook it by granting a pardon to the offender. It appeals to "mysteries" by insisting we accept the meaningless to save ourselves. Many have tried to do this by forming cults of worship in elder brother's name.

Forgiveness through the Holy Spirit is looking beyond the error from the beginning. This keeps it false for us. We must not let any belief that it is valid enter our mind or we think we have to undo the error to be forgiven. By always canceling out its effects, the Holy Spirit teaches that the ego does not exist, and proves it.

Forgiveness is the Holy Spirit's function. We should follow His teaching because He knows how to fulfill it perfectly. Miracles are a sign of our willingness to follow the Holy Spirit's plan of salvation, even though we do not understand what it is.

The ego's plan for forgiveness is based on the idea that the unhealed healer tries to give what he has not received for himself. Examples of this are:

- A theologian might say, "I am a miserable sinner and so are you."
- A psychotherapist might believe that attack is real for both himself and his patient, but that it does not matter for either of them.

Both these beliefs are equally absurd.

When we use the Atonement it will become real and visible to us. The ego believes it must use attack without forgiveness to ensure the guilt that holds all its relationships together. Forgiveness lies in communication. The Holy Spirit teaches those who believe communication is damnation that communication is salvation.

Listen to the Holy Spirit

We are afraid of forgiveness because we think it will lead to love and we are afraid of love. But our Friend, the Holy Spirit, will teach us to remember that forgiveness will release us. It is not loss but our salvation. When forgiveness is complete we will recognize that there is nothing to forgive. When we cannot hear the Holy Spirit's Voice it is because we are afraid of salvation. We think we will be punished first for the terrible sins we have committed. Our fear of God's Judgement on us leads us to listen to the ego, whose shrill voice overpowers His Voice.

But there is no sin. In our dreaming we selected the shadow figures we wanted to make immortal in the world we made. We put the shadow figures in the dream to prove our brother is guilty of doing what he did not do. We do not understand how they came into our mind and how we hear them. But they are only illusions. They symbolize the evil we think was done to us in the past. We bring them along to return evil for evil. In the past we hoped we could think guiltily of another and not bring harm to ourselves. But now we should be willing to forgive the Son of God for what he did not do. We want to release our brothers from the prison we have made by forgiving them for what they did not do.

Forgiveness enables the Holy Spirit, when He is invited, to bring His interpretation of the body as a means of communication into relationships. When all but loving thoughts has been forgotten, what is left is eternal. We will see the true loveliness of our brother shining in and all around him when our forgiveness is complete.

Let us look upon our brother with complete forgiveness, from which no error is excluded and nothing is kept hidden. If we try to hide anything and keep it from our forgiveness, we are trying to keep part of the ego's world as our guide. But if we are completely honest with the Holy Spirit, then there will never be a mistake anywhere we cannot overlook. Our sight will never be blocked by any suffering. We will recognize every illusion as a mistake, a shadow through which we will easily pass. God would let nothing interfere with those whose wills are the same as His. They will quickly remember what they are.

We attack our brother any time we withhold any part of our forgiveness. If we give nothing, then that is what we will receive. We cannot withhold forgiveness a little and expect it to be effective. We do not understand the meaning of love if we think we can attack for this and love for that. Forgiveness is the answer to any attack. Whenever we encounter hate, we should answer it in the name of love. Whoever has been injured by his brother should still love and trust him. Our imagined injury was caused by the ego, not by our brother. Our goal should be to undo the harm our ego has done to the other.

Forgiveness is the only function that is meaningful in time. The Holy Spirit uses it to translate sin into salvation. Forgiveness is for all and when everyone has salvation, it will be complete. Every function of this world will be completed with it and time will come to an end. Only forgiveness offers miracles. It is this world's equivalent of Heaven's justice. Let us forgive the past and let it go for it is no longer here with us and cannot harm us.

Forgiveness will take away the little gap standing between our brother and ourselves. It is the wish that we be joined with him. It is called "wish" because it still conceives of other choices. It is not in opposition to God's Will, therefor, it is in line with Heaven's wishes. It removes the obstacles we placed between the Heaven where we are and the *recognition* of where and what we are.

Forgiveness is not pity, which seeks to pardon only what it thinks is the truth. We cannot pardon our brother for our injury because we think we are the better of the two. His pardon and our belief that we are hurt cannot exist together. We should forgive our hurt first, then forgive our brother for what he did not do.

In true forgiveness, everything the observer looks on speaks to him of God. He sees no evil, nothing to fear and no one who is different from himself. Because he loves them, he can look on himself with love and gentleness. He looks with kindness on himself as he does on others. He does not condemn himself for his mistakes. Neither does he damn anyone else. He does not seek vengeance in the punishment of sin. He wants only to heal and bless.

To observe sin and still forgive it is a paradox. It says that what has been done to us does not deserve pardon. By giving pardon, we grant mercy to our brother while still keeping the proof he is not really innocent. Those who are sick are still accusers. They cannot forgive their brothers or themselves.

No one who has learned, and uses, true forgiveness can suffer. They do not hold proof of sin before their brother's eyes.

They have overlooked it and removed it from their own. Forgiveness cannot be for one and not for the other. Who forgives is healed and in his healing is the proof he has truly pardoned his brother. He keeps no trace of condemnation that he would still hold against himself or against any living thing.

Forgiveness should be seen as the normal reaction to a call for help that is issued because of distress that results from error. Forgiveness is the only sane response. The world pardons "sinners" sometimes. But it remains aware they have sinned. Therefor, in the eyes of the world, they do not deserve the forgiveness that it gives.

When we forgive, we understand that what we thought our brother did to us has not happened. We recognize that there was no sin and so all our sins are forgiven. We look at what we thought was our brother's transgression, see that we are seeing falsely and let the thought go.

If we are unforgiving then we have closed our mind. We have made a judgement and will not raise it up for scrutiny. Nothing can make us change our mind because we believe the distortion we have projected. The power of our mind allows us to steamroller reality with our own point of view.

When we forgive, the world is forgiving in return. When we have forgiven its trespasses it looks on us with forgiving eyes. Forgiveness plays a role in ending the belief in death and all the beliefs that rise from guilt.

Forgiveness translates the world of sin into a simple world where justice can be reflected from beyond Heaven's gate. What is charity in the world gives way to simple justice. We can forgive because we have believed in sin and we still believe we have a lot to be forgiven. Forgiveness thus becomes the means by which we learn we have done nothing that needs to be forgiven. Forgiveness always stays with the one who offers it, until he sees himself as needing it no more. Then he is returned to his real function of creating, which forgiveness offers again to him.

Forgiveness turns the world of sin into a world of glory. There is no sadness and no parting of brothers here. Everything has been totally forgiven and so has joined, each with the other, giving the oneness of the Sonship. There is no space standing between brothers to keep them separate. The sinless perceive they are one. In the space left vacant they join as one.

Forgiveness is not the end. It makes everything lovely but it does not create. It is the source of healing. It is the messenger of love, but not its Source. We are led here so God can take the final step, a step still further inward that we cannot take by ourselves. It transports us to the Source of light. Forgiveness removes what is not true from the world, carrying it to the bright world of clean and new perception. This is the real world.

The Real World

There is a different world that everyone will eventually find their way to. It is called the real world. It is all that the Holy Spirit has saved for us out of what we have made. When we find our way there, we will have achieved salvation. Salvation is God's promise that we will all find our way back to Him.

When we cross the little bridge between this world and the real world, the little spark holding the Great Rays is seen with the body's eyes for a time. The little spark will not stay little for long. We will come to realize the only value the body has is to be used to bring our brothers along so they can be released from prison with us at the bridge.

The ego always adds something to what is real, making it an illusion. We cannot tell what is real if we believe in both truth and illusions. We made a world to prove our personal independence from our Father. We believed we could make something separate from Him. Only what is true is like Him. If we perceive the real world only, we will be led to Heaven.

Real world- there is no sickness here. There is no separation and no division. Only loving thoughts are recognized. There is no death. Everything reflects the eternal. The world that God gave to his only begotten Son is the real world. He gave us the real world in exchange for the one we made.

The real world has no buildings. There are no streets where people walk alone and separate. There are no stores where people buy an endless list of "stuff" they do not need. There is no night with artificial light or day that grows bright and then dim. There is no loss. Everything here shines, and shines forever.

In the real world the stars disappear in the light. The sun, which opened the world to beauty, will vanish. Perception will be meaningless. Everything used for learning will not have a function anymore. Everything will be changeless. There will be no differences or variations in anything. Guilt meets with forgiveness here and fades away. The outside world is seen without the shadows of guilt on it.

When the real world is finally perceived we will find that our new perception will be quickly changed into knowledge. Then everything we made will be forgotten. The real world will disappear as Heaven and earth become one. When this world comes to an end it will not be through its destruction. It will be translated into Heaven.

When we have accepted ourselves without any falseness we will see the real world. Our Father will lean down to us then and take the last step for us by raising us up unto Himself.

Those we forgive will look more beautiful to us than we can possibly imagine. Nothing in our memory that made our heart sing with joy can come close to the happiness we will feel at this sight. We will see the Son of God in all the beauty the Holy Spirit loves to look upon. The Father created Him to see this for us until we learn to see it for ourselves. All the Holy Spirit's teaching leads to seeing this beauty and giving thanks with Him for it.

When we see this loveliness we will be looking upon the real world where everything is clean and new. Everything will sparkle under the sun. Everything has been given to God's Son here so nothing is hidden.

The real world is a state of mind. The only purpose it has is forgiveness. Its aim is the escape from guilt. Fear is not a goal and idols are no longer sought. No rules are set and no demands made on anyone. There is a wish to understand all created things as they really are. Now it is recognized that they must be forgiven before they can be understood.

In this world of the ego it is believed that understanding is acquired by attack. In the real world it becomes clear that understanding is lost by attack. The pursuit of guilt as a goal is recognized as foolishness. Idols are not wanted. Guilt is understood as the sole cause of pain. No one is tempted by its appeal because no one wants suffering and death. Freedom is seen as being possible and the world becomes a place of hope.

Its only purpose is to be a place where the hope of happiness can be realized. Everyone has this hope, for the world is united in the belief all must share in this purpose.

We are welcome in the real world. Our innocence waits there to cover us and make us ready for our final step in the journey inward. The dark, heavy garments of guilt will be replaced by purity and love.

Here is the end of the journey. Calling it the real world implies a limited reality, or partial truth, a small segment of the universe that has been made true. When knowledge and perception are brought together, only knowledge will continue past the gate. Salvation is a borderland where time, place and choice still have meaning. But they are temporary here, out of place. Every choice has already been made.

The little bridge between the real world and this world is the strongest thing touching this world. Yet it is easy to cross. This little step is a stride through time into eternity. It is a step from ugliness to the real world of perfect beauty. When we reach there, God will take the final step so swiftly we will have almost no time to thank Him for it.

Our Father, Who is in Heaven,
Your Name is holy, as is mine,
for I am Your Son.
Your Kingdom has come, It is here within me,
And I will not fear to look within,

Where I will lay the lilies of forgiveness
As my gift to You.

Let Your Will be done here on earth
as it is in Heaven.
Father, I want what it is not my will to have
And I do not want what it is my will to have.
Straighten out my mind, my Father, for it is sick.

And give me today your daily Word,
But forgive me for the mistakes I thought I made,
And let me forgive my brothers for what I thought they
did to me.

Let me not wander into the temptations
of this world,
But deliver me from the evil little self I made.
Amen

"He who cannot forgive others breaks the bridge over which he himself must pass."

George Herbert

Chapter 7

THE HOLY INSTANT AND THE HOLY RELATIONSHIP

Introduction

Everything we have been taught is completely wrong. Everything is upside-down in this world we think we live in. We made a world to indulge our fantasies but we did not allow for an easy way out of it, back to reality. But we can reverse our thinking and remember what we really are in just an instant of time. Time, without a past or present, is nothing, an illusion.

We can begin anytime to start practicing the Holy Spirit's use of time. We can take this instant, *now*, and embrace it as all there is of time. Nothing from the past can touch us if we decide that is what we really want. We are completely free, completely absolved and completely free of all condemnation in this very instant. This is a holy instant where holiness is reborn. We can go forward from here without fear and with no sense of change with time.

As described in Chapter 5, everyone has experienced the feeling of being transported beyond himself – transcending time and place. It is a sudden feeling of liberation from the body, a joining of something else in which our mind is enlarged. We unite with this something else as we become whole. The fear of union is gone and love instantly replaces it, extending to what freed us and uniting with it. We become certain of our identity. We have escaped from fear to peace, accepting reality without question. We let ourselves be one with something beyond the body, not letting our mind be limited by it. What we experienced is similar to a holy instant.

The Holy Instant

In the past we have never completely forgotten the body. But if we can become completely unaware of it for only an instant the miracle of the Atonement will happen. The body can never be seen quite the same after this. Each time we spend an instant without awareness of the body, we will have a different view of it when we return.

The body does not exist in any single instant. It is never experienced just *now.* Its past is remembered or its future is anticipated, making it seem real. It is controlled entirely by time. The way to escape time is to realize that there is no attraction for guilt in the *now* of the present. If guilt is experienced in any single instant, it is only imaginary.

To accept the holy instant without reservation we have to be willing to see no past or future. If we prepare for it then we place it in the future. The instant we desire it we will be released. Many have spent a lifetime in preparation but very few have had instants of success because they anticipate the future.

It is not necessary to follow a long, tedious path to atonement. We do not need to spend a lifetime fighting sin, or in contemplation, or meditation aimed at detachment from the body. These attempts will ultimately succeed, but they are tedious and time consuming. They all look to the future for release from the present state of unworthiness and inadequacy instead of concentrating on the *now*.

The holy instant will happen to everyone, but we have to practice it. All we need do is relax, be perfectly still, and say to ourselves, "I need do nothing." When we become completely unaware of the body, it will happen. The more we practice, the more we will learn. When it happens, we will recognize it by its glittering brilliance. No other gift of God can be recognized in any other way, it will blind us to this world.

We can start practicing separating out the holy instant *now*. If we become perfectly still then we will receive specific instructions for our little part in it. We will begin to experience a feeling of oneness when we learn to separate it out and experience it as timeless. God's Teacher and His lesson will support our strength in this. It is the practice of the power of God in us. It waits beyond the past and future to release us from the littleness we think we are.

For a while we may be tempted to bring illusions into the holy instant. This attempt to hinder our experience of the difference between truth and illusions will not be for long. Our illusions will prevent us from keeping the experience in our mind., but the power of the Holy Spirit will prevail. The holy instant is timeless and our illusions about time can not prevent us from experiencing the eternal.

Holiness does not change but time does. In the holy instant hell does not exist. Heaven is there instead. It is like a small picture of Heaven set in a frame of time. Heaven will not change because God will not change. The birth into the holy present is the way we are saved from things that change. God is remembered in the holy instant.

Our problem is not how long it will take to completely change our mind from wanting hell to wanting Heaven instead. That will be done in an instant by the Holy Spirit. The problem we have is – how long will it take to teach ourselves to be *willing* to give Him this tiny instant. He offers Heaven in exchange for it but we are afraid we will have to "sacrifice" everything we think we own in this world.

First, we have to be willing to give this holy instant to the Holy Spirit on behalf of our brothers. Then, and only then, will we be willing to give it to Him on our own behalf. We cannot have the instant of holiness alone, it must be shared. When we are tempted to attack a brother, we should remember that the instant he is released, so are we. If we offer a miracle of love, then we offer an instant of release, showing we are willing to be released.

Let us practice giving the holy instant to all who are slaves of time. The Holy Spirit gives their blessed instant to us as we give it to them because we share the Holy Spirit with our brothers. And let us be willing to give what we want to receive from Him. All of our guilt feelings are released in the holy instant.

Elder Brother in the Holy Instant

What can happen in an instant? We can:

- Re-establish perfect sanity, peace and love for everyone, for God and for ourselves.
- Remember immortality and our immortal creations.
- Exchange hell for Heaven.

- Transcend all of the ego's works and ascend unto our Father.

There may be a tendency to be afraid of the holy instant. Instead, we should welcome it because there is no fear in it. It is eternal and comes to us from God through His Teacher. He translates time into eternity. In the holy instant we stand before God's altar through Him. In that instant we will see the holy altar on which our Father has placed Himself. He translates hell into Heaven, our home, where God wants us to be.

We are where God would have us be. The holy instant reaches out to embrace time as God reaches out to embrace us. We have spent enormous amounts of time tying our brothers to our egos in support of the ego's weaknesses. In the holy instant we release our brothers and refuse to support their weaknesses or our own.

It is wrong for us to use our brothers in support of our egos. We use them to give us excuses for not letting it go. But, if we let them, they offer far stronger support for the Holy Spirit in us. It is up to us whether they support the ego or the Holy Spirit. It will be clear which we have chosen by their reaction to us. If we are not certain, it is because we have not given a holy instant to the Holy Spirit. When we have, we will be absolutely certain.

The goal here is to diminish the value the body has for us until it is down to nothing. Then there will be no interference with communication. Our thoughts will be as free as God's. We can achieve this if we reject the use of the body for separation and attack. We will come to realize that we do not need the body at all. Bodies do not exist in the holy instant. We will be left to experience the attraction for God and we will join Him wholly, in an instant. Any time we are willing to give over every plan but His, we can claim the holy instant. But we must want it wholly, without reservation.

Standing within the holy instant is our elder brother. How we accept him and his teaching determines how soon we will experience the holy instant. He wants us to accept the holy instant *now*, this instant. We should always keep in mind that our acceptance depends on willingness, not time.

The Conditions For Love

The holy instant is the Holy Spirit's most useful aid in teaching us the meaning of love. Its purpose is to suspend judgement. We base our judgement on past experience. Without the past– i.e. without the ego – judgement is impossible. Without it we do not understand anything. This causes us to be afraid because we think that without the ego everything would be chaos. In reality, without the ego everything would be love. The ego is always trying to block our feelings of love.

God knows no special love so love is not special. We cannot love any differently than He does and still understand the meaning of love. Our belief in special relationships with special love shows we still believe in separation as our salvation. Salvation depends on everyone being equal in receiving the Atonement. In the past we taught ourselves that special parts of the Sonship could give us more than others. In the holy instant we will learn that this is false teaching.

The Holy Spirit knows how to bring a touch of Heaven to our relationships. In the holy instant no one is special. Our brothers will all seem the same as each other and the same as ourselves when we see them without the values from the past.

We will see no separation between brothers. We will see each relationship as it is in reality when we perceive only the present.

In the holy instant we know that real love is in us because we become free of the past with its strange ideas of love. We do not have to snatch love guiltily from a source external to us. Love has no meaning apart from the meaning God gave it. God loves everyone equally. He needs everyone equally, and so do we.

In the holy instant we unite directly with God and all our brothers in Christ. Christ is the Self the Sonship shares and God shares His Self with Christ. The holy instant extends to eternity and to the Mind of God. Love has meaning only in God's Mind and can be understood only there.

Gain and loss are both accepted in this world of scarcity. Love is meaningless here. No one is aware they have perfect love within. In the holy instant we hold all our brothers in our mind where we experience no loss, only completion; which is love under the laws of God. In the holy instant only the laws of God prevail. The laws of this world become meaningless. When the Son of God accepts the laws of God he will no longer be a prisoner in the world of sin.

The veil of time is lifted in the holy instant. We become aware that reality never changes. Until this happens we cannot have faith in love without fear. The holy instant will be given to us through our elder brother by the Holy Spirit. After that, we will also give it, for the Sons of God share a need for it. We will have joined with elder brother and will be able to offer the holy instant with him to everyone.

God is remembered in the holy instant. The language of communication with all our brothers is remembered also. No one is excluded. The past is gone so everyone is seen now as sinless. God and the power of God will be within us and we will begin to understand what our Creator is.

In the holy instant minds are joined without the body's interference. This is the condition needed for love. Where there is communication, there is peace. If the body were to be destroyed, communication would still continue in the condition of love. The realization that to sacrifice the body is nothing will come. Communication cannot be sacrificed because it is of the mind. Our elder brother teaches us that there is no sacrifice and love is everywhere, always.

A New Look at Relationships

After we have experienced the holy instant we will still need the Holy Spirit's teaching. He will not leave us to be our own teachers until the holy instant has extended far beyond time. He uses everything in this world for our release. We are afraid of forgiveness, so He will teach us to remember that forgiveness will release us.

Forgiveness is not loss but salvation. When forgiveness is complete, we will recognize there is nothing to forgive. To open our mind to His teaching, we need merely ask the Holy Spirit to teach us how to forgive.

The ego wants us to see our brothers as being nothing more than a body. The Holy Spirit wants us to see the Great Rays shining from our brothers. This shift in vision will happen in the holy instant. When we learn how to achieve this shift we will want to make it permanent. Then we will want to accept it as the only perception we desire. It will be translated into knowledge by God Himself as part of the Atonement. When we achieve this we will have transcended the ego.

The Great Rays will replace our awareness of the body in the holy instant. Then we can recognize unlimited relationships. Every use the ego has for the body can be given up by us because we share no purpose with it. If we think we do, we will use the body to limit everyone as we follow the ego's instructions. The ego's purposes can never be achieved, but it will strive for them with all the strength we give it. Let us decide to ignore the ego's strident calls to attack. Instead, let us offer our brothers only love thoughts and deeds.

We all have much to do in reversing our thinking. This world is old and tired and is crumbling at the seams. Let each of us accept the holy instant and take our place in the Great Awakening with our elder brother. As this year is born, let us make it different by making it all the same. By offering each one we meet perfect forgiveness, all our relationships will be made holy for us.

Each instant, coupled with the next instant, and then the next, stretches off into eternity. We see each holy instant as a different point in time. All it ever held or will hold is here, right *now*. The past takes nothing from it. The future will add nothing to it. Here is perfect faith, the loveliness of a relationship, the means and end in perfect harmony. One day we, in our turn, will offer the faith already offered to us. Here is the limitless forgiveness we will give each other, the face of Christ we will look upon.

Whenever our thoughts wander to a special relationship which still tempts us, we should enter into a holy instant with the Holy Spirit. He needs only our willingness to release us. Our willingness need not be complete. His perfect faith will make up for our lack of willingness. He will give us his perfect willingness to replace our little willingness. If we call on Him then He will call on Heaven for us. Heaven is at His call.

The holy instant shines the same on all relationships, for they are all one in it. Healing is there, already complete and perfect. God is there, and where He is only the perfect can be.

The Holy Relationship

Bodies serve no useful purpose. When used as the Holy Spirit teaches they have no function. True communication is by minds only, not by bodies. The sight that sees the body has no use in a holy relationship. It takes only one holy instant to begin a holy relationship. It is a little breath of eternity that runs through time. Nothing is before it and nothing afterwards. Nothing will ever be the same in our sight afterwards.

The holy instant is not remembered without an expression of praise. In the holy relationship we are constantly reminded of the experience when the relationship was born. The unholy relationship is a continuous hymn of hate in praise of the ego and its home, the body. The holy relationship is a happy song of praise to the Redeemer of relationships. In the holy relationship we will know our own Identity, exchange our doubts for certainty, be free of misery and learn again of joy.

The holy relationship has to be learned. It is a major step toward perceiving the real world. It represents the reversal of the unholy relationship, transforming it so it is seen as new. The only difficult part is the beginning. First, we offer the relationship to the Holy Spirit for the purpose of holiness. The first result of this is that the goal of the relationship is abruptly reversed.

He immediately accepts our invitation and replaces our goal with His. This makes the relationship seem disturbed and quite distressing. The problem is, the relationship is out of line with its own goal. The old goal was all that seemed to make sense in this insane world, in its unholy state. Many relationships have been broken off at this point because the old goal did not make sense anymore. A new relationship is often sought to re-establish the old goal. But once an unholy relationship has accepted the goal of holiness it can never return to what it once was.

The goal must be shifted abruptly. If it were not, the ego would have time to reinterpret each step to its liking. Both members of the relationship must prepare themselves for this very important change. With a radical shift in purpose, a complete change of mind of what the relationship is for occurs. Two individuals who started an unholy relationship for the purpose of sin suddenly have a goal of holiness. Inevitably, they are appalled at the new purpose because they do not perceive the relationship rationally.

The Holy Spirit can translate our special relationships into holiness by removing as much fear as we will let Him. If we are willing to place the relationship under His care, He will remove all pain from it. If we let go of our imagined needs, He will remove all fear from it. He knows no one is special.

Faith is needed at this point. It was an act of faith when we let our goal be set for us. We need faith now that we are about to receive the rewards of our original faith. We believed the Holy Spirit was there to accept the relationship. Now we must have faith that He is still there to purify it. And we must keep faith in our brother in a trying time. We now know we are in an insane relationship but we are striving for sanity as its purpose. Many mistakes have been made since we invited the Holy Spirit in. We may blame our brother for any discomfort in the relationship. We must be careful to not lose sight of the holy instant because of this.

In the holy instant we are joined with many of our brothers. God Himself has blessed our holy relationship. We need to welcome salvation together by blessing each other and our relationship. Salvation comes to us in our relationship and all the Sonship is blessed. Time can close over the experience of an instant. It is easily forgotten if we are not careful and make a conscious effort to keep it foremost in our mind. If we attack our brother or use judgement in any way we neutralize the effects of the holy instant.

Everyone has received the gift of a holy instant at some time. But we may have set up a set of conditions in which it was not usable. Therefor, we did not recognize it was with us at the time. Every time we attack a brother or judge him we reinforce this condition.

We start to recognize the gifts we have given our brother when we experience a holy instant. We also begin to accept the effects of the holy instant. We can use these to correct our mistakes and free ourselves from their consequences. When we learn this lesson, we will have learned how to free the Sonship.

As a holy relationship develops, our faith in the Holy Spirit is strengthened because we realize He is always with us to help us in any situation. We are no longer wholly insane or alone. We cannot be alone in God and we will come to know that He is with us in our new relationship. Loneliness has departed from our holy relationship. The truth has come to call us to salvation and peace. The strong call of truth will reinforce our faith.

Everyone has been called by God to return to Heaven, our home. It is the most holy function in this world. It is offered to us and we will hear it in a holy relationship. Our simple task is to accept it and offer it to our brothers. It will reach out to heal every broken fragment of the Sonship. We are given the peace of God and the holy light that brought us together will extend from us to everyone.

A holy relationship is a miracle and contains every miracle. Each miracle is a gentle winning over from the appeal of guilt to the appeal of love. There is no order of difficulty in miracles, they are all the same. The One Who answered our call is in our holy relationship. We must be careful or we will interfere with His holy purpose. Let Him extend the miracle of our relationship to everyone in it.

As long as we stay dedicated to our holy relationship the body will stay perfect and healthy while it is used for our holy purpose. The body no more dies than it has feelings. It is neither corruptible nor incorruptible. We gave the body to the Holy Spirit for His use as a training device and in His sight it is neutral, incapable of being sick or in pain.

We keep trying to make the Son of God adjust to the insanity of the ego. We should keep in mind that an evil intruder invaded the home of truth. He cannot remain before the shining light the Holy Spirit offered us and we accepted. We should not ask this intruder who we are because in all the universe he is the one thing that does not know the answer. But we try to adjust to his answer even though he is the only blind thing in the seeing universe.

The world we see is the answer we got. We gave the ego power to adjust the world, trying to make its answer true. We asked this mad thing for the meaning of our unholy relationship. We made adjustments according to its insane answer. But that did not make us happy. We did not meet the Son of God with joy and bless him, nor did we give thanks for the happiness he held out to us. We were blind to the holiness shining in both of us because we did not recognize our brother as the eternal gift of God to us. The purpose of our holy relationship cannot be kept from us by the one thing that wants to keep it unholy.

The Son of God comes closest to himself in a holy relationship. He starts to find the certainty of purpose his Father has in him. He assumes his role of restoring God's laws and of what has been lost. Only in time can anything be lost, and never forever. The parts of the Son of God will gradually join in time. The end of time is brought nearer with each joining. In the holy relationship there is a preview of eternity with each miracle of joining. And all fear, the foundation of this world, is gone.

The holy relationship reflects the true relationship of the Son of God with his Father. The Holy Spirit resides in it and Love smiles on it. In it we are on the path that leads us home. We walk together in it, leaving the body behind. Love's Everlasting Arms receive us, giving us peace forever.

We will be given the means to achieve this happy end. When we see our brothers as sinless we will be given both the means and the end. All is given to those who ask to see and have given complete forgiveness. We can only give what we have received and we will have received complete forgiveness.

The body's eyes adjust to sin and see it every where, in everything. The holy relationship is in danger when seen through the body's eyes and will lose its meaning if great care is not exercised. Each one must look within and see no lack. He extends his completion by joining another who is as whole as himself. He can see no difference between them so there is nothing he wants to take for himself. Now they know their own reality as they stand just under Heaven, close enough not to return to this world.

In Heaven there are no differences. In a holy relationship faith in differences is shifted to faith in sameness. Reason leads us to the logical conclusion of our union with our brother. It must extend, as we extended when we joined, to reach out beyond itself. The sameness we now see extends and removes all differences. There always was this sameness underneath the differences and it becomes apparent now. We will find here a golden circle where we recognize the Son of God. What is born into a holy relationship will never end.

Christ will come to what is like Himself. He is always drawn to a holy relationship, which is like Him. That which draws us together in holiness attracts Him to us. In the holy relationship His sweetness and gentleness is protected from attack. We make Him welcome, for faith in one another is faith in Him. It is correct to look on each other as His chosen home. Our will is His Will here as it is our Father's. Who is drawn to Christ is drawn to God as surely as they both are drawn to every holy relationship. It is the home prepared for Them as earth is transformed into Heaven.

Our minds will act as one in the holy relationship as we experience what the other is thinking. We should not be fearful of this happy fact. By accepting it, we will come to realize our relationship reflects the union of the Creator and His Son. Every thought in one loving mind brings gladness to the other.

Each shining thought of love extends its presence, creating more of itself.

A holy relationship is beloved of God Himself. It is immortal on earth. Great power lies in it as time waits on its will. All separation is gone from the earth as all illusions are brought to forgiveness and disappear, Christ is reborn at its center, to light His home and the world with His vision. Joy will replace all misery. Is this not the home we want?

"The Bible tells us to love our neighbors, and also our enemies, probably because they are the same people."

G.K. Chesterton

Chapter 8

IT TAKES TWO

Introduction

In our natural state we will not live out a little life in a body. Our real nature is spiritual, with all the power God gave us when He created us. Everyone is searching to find himself and the power and the glory he knows subconsciously that he has lost. They are there and can be found whenever we are with a brother. The ego, not knowing where to look, tries to find power and glory in an alliance with the body. The Holy Spirit teaches we can find our savior only in our brother.

When we are with a brother we teach each other what we think we are. We will see in him either pain or joy depending on which teacher we listen to. What we see is our acceptance of his belief in what he thinks he is, and what he sees is his acceptance of what we think we are. Both will be imprisoned in this world of sin or freed according to our decisions. We will see our savior when we look on our brother as sinless.

"Revenge is a kind of wild justice, which the more man's nature runs to, the more ought law to weed it out". Francis Bacon

Our elder brother will deny us nothing on our journey back to God. When fear intrudes, it is the ego trying to join the journey. It cannot and feels rejected. It tries to retaliate but cannot bring harm to us because elder brother is there to protect us. We chose him instead of the ego. However, if we try to hold on to both, we will lose our way.

We are Our Brother's Savior

Our elder brother was taught to travel in one direction only by the Holy Spirit. But illusions can obscure this singleness of purpose, so the ego must not be given the power to interfere with our journey. Because we want to transcend the ego we must leave all illusions behind. If we reach our hand out to our elder brother, he will take it and guide us as he goes before us beyond the ego. His strength will never fail and, if we choose to share in it, he will gladly help us. He gives it willingly because he needs us as much as we need him.

When we are angry with a brother it is because we believe we can save the ego by attack. If we think that he is attacking, we are agreeing with his belief that he can save the ego. If we attack him, we are reinforcing the belief in ourselves. Attack is really a call for help; our brother needs our gift of love, not our anger or attack. That is the way out of prison for both of us.

We are not separated from God or from each other. God created our reality and there is no substitute for it. Together

---

A little philosophy inclineth man's mind to atheism, but depth in philosophy bringeth men's minds about to religion. Francis Bacon with our brother we are so firmly joined in truth that only God is there. God is with us and He loves us both, equally and as one.

The Son of God cannot be driven by external events. What happens to him is always his choice – in every situation his power of decision is in control. No accident or chance is possible within the universe as God created it. And there is nothing outside it. If we suffer, we have decided sin was our goal. If we decide to be happy, then we have given the power of decision and left all judgements to the Holy Spirit.

We are our brother's savior and he is ours. There is much love in this plan, which was given to it by Love. The plan is set up to have us learn what we must be. Let us accept what is given to us to give to our brother. Together we can learn what has been given to us. To give is no more blessed than to receive. Neither is it less, we can receive only when we give.

We must be careful not to desert our brother now. We are all the same; we will not decide alone or differently from each other. We give each other either life or death. We are each other's savior or judge, offering either sanctuary or condemnation. We will either escape from misery entirely or not at all. Reason will tell us that we cannot pause in some middle ground, waiting to choose between the misery of hell or the joy of Heaven. We are in hell and miserable on earth until we choose Heaven.

No One is Special

Here is our role in the universe: The Lord of Love and Life has entrusted all salvation from the misery of hell to every part of true creation. Each one has the grace to be a savior to the holy ones entrusted to him. He learns this for himself when he first looks on a brother as he looks on himself and sees the mirror of himself there. The concept of his self is laid aside. Nothing can stand between his sight and what he looks on, to judge what he beholds. He sees the face of Christ in this single vision. He comes to understand that he looks on everyone as he beholds this one. Light is there where darkness was before. Now the veil is lifted from his sight.

When we have lifted the veil together, we will free more than just the two of us. We become the saviors of the world, walking the world with God by our side and carrying His message of hope to everyone who needs a miracle to save them.

What our brother thinks we are shows us what we believe is our reality. Each one is released as he sees his brother as sinless and looks on him as his savior instead of the attacker he thought was there. That is our function here, our part in bringing peace to all. Let us not try to substitute another goal but serve this one willingly.

The ego makes comparisons to emphasize separateness. Love makes no comparisons. Specialness always compares itself with others to maintain itself. A comparison is established by a lack in another. It keeps all lacks it perceives before its awareness. When we think we see a lack, we are maligning our savior. We have made him small compared to our specialness, making us seem to stand straight and tall in comparison. But it is ourselves we are maligning.

The pursuit of specialness is always at the cost of our peace. We cannot attack our savior and still recognize his support for us. We cannot detract from his omnipotence and still share his power. The pursuit of salvation will bring us joy. The pursuit of specialness will bring us pain. The goal of specialness runs counter to the Will of God and would defeat salvation. If we value specialness then we value an illusion of ourselves more than we value the truth.

Our brother is our savior and has the power to forgive us all the sins we think we placed between him and his function of salvation. The truth is the same in both of us, we cannot change it, but we both can understand it. It can bring release to us both. Our brother holds the key to Heaven out to us. But the dream of specialness is obscuring it from our sight.

If we look on our brother as a friend, we will see all the loveliness within ourselves. He is the enemy of specialness but friend to what is real within. Our attacks on him have not affected the gift God gave him to give to us. He needs to give it and we need to receive it. Let him forgive all our specialness and make us whole in mind and one with him. He is waiting for our forgiveness so he may return it to us.

Our brother is the same as we are. He is not special, but has everything, including us. We should not hold back the gift of ourselves to him. Remember God gave Himself to both in equal love so both could share the universe with Him.

As soon as we recognize our brother's holiness the world becomes still, filled with peace and with no conflict anywhere. We are looking at our promise that God is here with us now and are certain that God is knowable and will be known to us. In our brother we see God's creation. Christ is there each time we look on our brother. But our eyes are closed and we cannot find our savior by trying to see through sightless eyes.

The wish to see invites the grace of God upon our eyes. It brings the gift of light that makes sight possible. If we remember that God wills we recognize our savior then we will want to truly see our brother. Our brother will remain lonely as long as he is not fulfilling the function God gave him.

The Son of God asks that we return to him what is his due, so we can share it with him. It is useless to both when we are alone. It gives equal strength to both when we are together, the sum is far greater than the parts. Our savior offers salvation when we forgive him but he offers death when we condemn him. God has not condemned His Son, but we have.

Everyone we see is a reflection of what we want him to be to us. If we decide we do not like him, that makes him not worthy of the role God gave him and we deprive him of the joy he would have by fulfilling that role. And Heaven is not lost to him alone, we are also deprived by being kept from our natural home. It can be regained only if we show him the way by deciding we love him and seeing him as sinless. We will find it together, walking side by side, with love as our companion.

The body cannot be used for union. When we see our brother as a body we have set up a state where union with him is not possible. By seeing him as a body we have not had faith that he was the Son of God and this faithlessness to him has separated us. It has kept us both from being healed by bringing illusions to stand between us.

Instead of seeing a body, we should give faith, hope, love and mercy to each other. God has given us a gift in our brother, waiting there for us to receive it. We can be savior and give redemption to each other. If we share in redemption we will rise to Heaven together with our elder brother and not be separate in death.

Let us look lovingly on our brother and see in him the reversal of the laws that rule this world. Our freedom can be seen in him if we do not let his specialness obscure the truth in him. If we bind him to one law of death from the world of the ego then we will not escape the same sentence. Every sin we see in him keeps us both in hell. But if we see his perfect sinlessness we both will be released.

Healing by Joining

It takes only two who want happiness to offer it to the world. It takes only two to understand they cannot decide alone. It takes only two to guarantee the joy they asked for will be wholly shared. There is a basic law that makes decision powerful and gives them all their effects. It is:

It only takes two who are joined in spirit to make a decision come true.

Before there can be a decision, two must join into a holy relationship. If we keep this in mind then we will have the happiness we want. We will give it to the world because we had it ourselves and we can give only what we have ourselves. Our decision for a happy day lifts our judgement from the world. As we give, so will we receive in return.

Where two have joined hands, the Will of God resides there forever. They thought He was their enemy until they joined. When they joined and shared a purpose, they learned their will was one and the same. They became aware of the Will of God. Now they will always remember that it is only what they desire now and forever more.

We have a subconscious wish to be treated unfairly, which comes from the ego. It is an attempt at compromising our desire for attack and our basic innocence. Since they are incompatible they cannot join and the attempt causes a stressful situation and we become fearful. If we are unfairly treated, our brother also suffers from the unfairness we see. Both of us are crucified because we cannot crucify ourselves alone. We cannot sacrifice ourselves alone either. Sacrifice is total – if it were possible, the whole of God's creation would be involved, and the Father with His Son.

When we offer a miracle to our brother we are both released from guilt because we wished him well. When healing occurs it cannot look upon specialness – that is the law. Healing comes from love, not pity. Love proves that all suffering is only a foolish wish without any effects. Good health results from our desire to see our brother with only love in his heart. We will see what we wish for. We look out upon what we feel within, that is the law of seeing.

Healing happens when two minds think as one and call to all the Sonship to share in their joy. God goes into them and through them. Spirit obeys only the laws of God and so holds everything by giving it. The higher level of our mind thinks as spirit does and knows that if we give an idea away, we still keep it. Further, the one who accepts it, reinforces it in the mind of the giver. Since the world is one of ideas, giving cannot involve losing. Whatever we give to our brother is a gift to ourselves because we are all one.

When we have reached another mind and joined with it we will have succeeded in performing miracles. A miracle is merely an exposing of what was already there but not seen with the body's eyes. This is the first link in the joining of the awareness of the Sonship. The joining happens when we put ourselves under the guidance of the Holy Spirit. We should not try to force the joining or try to understand what has happened or we will not be convinced of its reality. No two minds can join in the desire for love without love joining them.

Our brother's worth to us is beyond our estimation. His Father established his worth and we will see it shining in him when we receive our Father's gift of love from him. We will not want to judge him because when we see the face of Christ shining in our brother, judgement is meaningless. We can choose either vision or judgement. If we choose vision we have accepted him as our savior and not judged him.

We can look again at our brother standing beside us and see that this is our friend and savior who we released from crucifixion with our vision. He is free now to lead us where he wants to be. We walk the way of innocence together, singing together in happiness as we see the open door of Heaven, our home. Let us give freely and gladly to one another the freedom and strength to lead each other there. Let us come before each other's holy altar where we will find the strength and freedom waiting there that is our inheritance. Both of us will be led past fear to love as the light shines in us for one another. Let us see our brother as sinless and we will share with him the power of the release from sin we offered to him.

Everyone who seems to walk this world alone has a special savior whose function here is to release him, and thus free himself. Each one will find his savior when he is ready to

---

And you must love him, ere to you
He will seem worthy of your love.
William Wordsworth

look upon the face of Christ in his brother by seeing him as sinless.

Each of us must seek only the Kingdom, because that is where the laws of God operate absolutely. They are the laws of truth. There is nothing else, God is All in all because all being is in Him Who is all Being. We are in Him for our being is His. By not recognizing the ego in our brother we strengthen the Holy Spirit in both of us and allow love to enter.

"Knowledge is gained by learning, trust by doubt, skill by practice and love by love."

Thomas Szasz

Chapter 9

ACCEPTING THE ATONEMENT

Introduction

Our part in God's Plan for salvation is already set. When we are forgiven we will join in the Atonement plan by giving forgiveness to every living thing in return. The wish to join with every living thing will establish our place. We will join with our elder brother for the salvation of all of God's creations by way of the miracle. Each miracle brings everyone closer to the Atonement. When the Atonement, as described in Chapter 2, occurs everyone will realize at last that they already have everything.

When we decide to change our mind about the way we are, then, with each relationship, each day we will be born again. Atonement will be enough to free us from the past. We should give our minds peacefully to the Atonement. When everyone is as welcome to us as we want to be welcome to our Father, our guilt will be gone. We will have accepted the Atonement. It was shining in us all the while we dreamed of guilt and we would not look within.

Guilt is always insane, there is no reason for it. While we believe there is a reason for guilt it will not end. We have to examine the source of our guilt to dispel it. While we see guilt in anyone for any reason, we will not look within and find the Atonement because we are merely projecting our own guilt outward onto our brother. The purpose of the Atonement is to dispel our illusions, not to see them as real and forgive them.

How Healing is Achieved

When we are healed, the Holy Spirit has saved us from what is now gone – the guilt. We no longer give reality to guilt by seeing a reason for it. The Holy Spirit teaches healing to us and He wants us to teach healing through Him. The Holy Spirit is in everyone's mind and is shared by all so what is learned by anyone is taught throughout the Sonship.

We can learn to use *now* to heal and teach. Forget the past and place the future in the hands of God. We think we are alone and lost in a dark and dangerous world full of pain. This is not what the world is *now*. What the body's eyes see is only the past, not the present. When we look within we will see a radiance there. This light is a reflection of the Love of God. To feel God's Love within is to see a new world, shining in innocence and alive with hope. It will seem incredible that we thought our Father did not love us. When we realize guilt is not justified and without reason, we will look upon and accept the Atonement.

We do not remember how much our Father loves us, or how much we love Him. When we made the ego, we blanked these memories out but they are still there, waiting for us to choose to remember. We are unmerciful to ourselves and our brothers because of this. When we look past the cloud of guilt dimming our vision we will see the lovely truth shining within. Christ is within us and He would have us see the altar to our Father in the holy place where we will see the light. Nothing can keep us from seeing the altar. It is as pure as He Who raised it to Himself. Christ offers mercy to all God's children. He wants us to also offer mercy to ourselves and our brothers. He wants us to see a world filled with perfect charity and love.

The only way to look within and see the light of love is to release ourselves from guilt as we want to be released ourselves. We who have always loved the Father can have no fear to look within because love is guiltless. The Holy Spirit will restore reason to us by removing all illusions from our sight. Reason will tell us that our guilt is without reason. It is not in the Mind of God, where we are, so it cannot possibly exist. The Holy Spirit will show us the perfect purity shining in ourselves through Christ's vision.

We cannot have real relationships with any of God's Sons unless we love them all and equally. Love is not special. If we single out part of the Sonship for our love then we impose guilt on all our relationships, and they become unreal or illusionary. We can love only the same way God does because we are part of Him and He is part of us. There is no love apart from His. We will never have any idea what love is like until we recognize this.

Anyone who condemns a brother cannot see himself as guiltless and as having the peace of God. If he is really guiltless and at peace then he could never condemn. He must be deluding himself and not looking within. Condemnation comes from comparison and love holds no comparisons. All brothers are the same in the sight of God and are loved equally by Him.

God gave us the Holy Spirit to remove all doubts and traces of guilt we have laid upon ourselves. The Holy Spirit's mission cannot fail. What God Wills, will be done. We *will* find the peace we were created in. God is invariable and He will not change His Mind about our peace.

We cannot give what we do not have. If we offer our blessing, it must have been given to us first. To give it we must have accepted the Atonement and learned we are guiltless. Miracles are happening constantly and they show that we are blessed. Miracles are part of the Atonement and occur whenever we smile on a brother, help another or any act of kindness that we do. A Miracle corrects the false illusion the body's eyes look upon and reminds the mind that perception is upside down. It is a correction that stays within times limits but paves the way for the return of timelessness.

When we forgive, we are forgiving all the illusions we held against our brothers. We are releasing them from the slavery of their illusions by forgiving them for the illusions we perceived in them. Forgiveness is part of the Atonement also and we should learn to practice it always. Forgiveness is the wish to join with our brother. To forgive is to remember only the loving thoughts that were given to us and those we gave to others.

Only illusions can be forgiven because our reality has no past. God is not able to have illusions so He holds nothing against anyone. We will learn we have been forgiven when we forgive our brothers for the illusions we offered them. This is all done in the holy instant, which will happen if we practice it every day..

When we are willing to give everything we held outside of truth to the Holy Spirit then it will be done. We do not do it, He does. It needs only our willingness to let go and let Him do it. If we lose our peace of mind because a brother is using fantasy to try to solve his problems, we are not forgiving ourselves for agreeing with his action. We are keeping both of us from salvation. If we forgive him then we restore to truth what we both denied to it. We will see forgiveness when and where we give it.

Those we forgive will look more beautiful to us than we can possibly imagine. Nothing in our memory that made us joyful will even come close to the happiness we will feel when we see our forgiven brothers. We will see the Son of God in all the beauty the Holy Spirit loves to look upon. The Father created Him to see this for us until we learn to see it for ourselves. When we see this beauty we will find the happiness we have been searching for since time began. All the Holy Spirit's teaching leads to seeing this beauty and giving thanks to Him for it.

The holy instant, the holy relationship and the Holy Spirit would have no purpose if we understood the difference between truth and illusion. All the means by which salvation is achieved are only parts of the plan to change our dreams of fear to happy dreams from which we will wake to knowledge. We are preparing now for the undoing of what never was. We should not try to take charge of this. We should be patient and reserve our assessment of our progress. We have judged some of our greatest advances as failures and some of our furthest retreats as successes. We tend to become impatient with our apparent lack of progress. But we are constantly making progress when we practice the lessons we learn from books such as this and especially *A Course in Miracles®*.

The holy instant removes all fear and hatred from our mind. We should not try to remove them ourselves because that is the Holy Spirit's function. We should not try to overlook our guilt before we ask the Holy Spirit for help. That is His function. If we offer Him a little willingness He will remove all fear and hatred as we are forgiven. That is all. He will take our little faith, join it with His understanding, and build our part in the Atonement. Together we will build a ladder with Him which will rise to Heaven. We will not be alone in our easy ascent to Heaven. But we must invite the Holy Spirit into our awareness and keep no secrets from Him.

Our brother is crucified by sin and waits on us for his release from pain. If we offer him forgiveness then he will give it to us. Every grace in Heaven can be offered by us to each other and will be given to us by the Holy Spirit. What we give, we share. Redemption has been given to us to give to each other. Let us forgive all the sins our brother thinks he has committed. Let us forgive all the guilt we think we see in him. Forgiveness is the end of specialness. Illusions disappear when they are forgiven. Forgiveness is the release from all illusions.

It is impossible to partly forgive. We cannot see ourselves as sinless if we cling to one illusion as still being lovely. We cannot give forgiveness wholly because we cannot receive it for ourselves. Our secret guilt would disappear the instant we wholly forgave because we would be forgiving ourselves.

Forgiveness is not real unless both are healed. We must first believe that our brother's sins do not affect us to demonstrate they are not real. His innocence can be attested to only if his sins have not caused any guilt. Sins are beyond forgiveness because they would have effects that could not be undone. In their undoing is the proof they were only errors made by illusions. We should let ourselves be healed so we may be forgiving and offer salvation to both our brother and ourselves.

A sick body shows the mind has not been healed. But a miracle of healing shows separation has no effect. We will be what we are able to prove to our brother. Everything we say or do or think affirms what we teach our brother. Our body can be the means to teach that it has never suffered pain because of him. It can offer him proof of his own innocence and offer him proof of his forgiveness.

A miracle offers the same to both ourselves and our brother. Our mind has been healed and has forgiven him for what he did not do. He becomes convinced his innocence was never lost and he is healed at the same time as we are. The miracle undoes all things the world claims cannot be undone. Death and hopelessness will disappear before the powerful call to life. The ancient calling of the Father to the Son, and the Son to his own, will be the last trumpet call the world will ever hear. We learn there is no death when we show our brother he did not hurt us. He thinks our blood is on his hands, so he thinks he stands condemned. But we can show him, by our healing, his guilt is only the fabric of a senseless dream.

The Altar of God

Evil dreams are real to the dreamers when they are shared. If we forgive the dreamer and perceive that he is not the dream he made, then we will not share the dream. Then he cannot be part of ours, from which we both are free. We are the dream, not the dreamer. Forgiveness separates the dreamer from the evil dream. If we share an evil dream, we must believe we are that dream. If we withhold our support then the dream is gone. Love must come where the fear has left.

The past will be transformed, being made continuous with the present, the *now* of time. The reality of the present is increased. When a relationship is given to the Holy Spirit for the purpose of holiness, the spark of beauty hidden in the ugliness comes alive and springs into a beautiful blossom. Hatred is no longer remembered. Atonement's emphasis is on the past because separation must be undone where it was made.

Our sick thought system will be corrected by the light from the true Foundation of life. When we fear salvation, we are choosing death, darkness and perception instead of life, light and knowledge. To believe these can be reconciled is to believe God and His Son cannot. We are not of this world so the problem of who is in authority here has no meaning. Our kingdom was given to us from beyond this world. This world is left by truth, not by death and truth can be known by everyone.

Teaching and learning will aid us in changing our mind about the dream of a separated ego with a world that rests upon it. Our thoughts are all part of a thought system that shows us this world of the ego. We should renounce our role as guardian of this thought system and open it to our elder brother. He will gently correct it, take us by the hand and lead us back to God and our home in Heaven.

To the Holy Spirit the world the ego made is a teaching device that He will use for bringing us back to our home. Our part is to correct our errors and learn His lessons. The Holy Spirit is always in direct communication with God as He is with us because He is part of us. He holds the remembrance of the past and of the future and brings them to the present. This is our guide to salvation. His goal is to increase our gladness by sharing it.

The Holy Spirit will help us out of fear by showing us that everything we perceive as fearful is just a lack of love. By joining in the Atonement we will escape our fears because we will learn that only what is loving is true. We can accept truth as part of ourselves because, as an extension of God, we created it with Him. Nothing that is good can be lost and nothing that is not good can be protected. The Kingdom's safety is guaranteed by the Atonement and the unified Sonship protects it. The ego fades away when we hear the Holy Spirit's call to be one with our brothers. We need our brothers, we cannot cancel out our past errors by ourselves.

The real world is in our mind. Our insane thoughts also are in our mind, splitting it into two thought systems. This is a dangerous situation and the mind resolves it by projecting the split – the antagonistic part – not the reality. We perceive this projected image as being antagonistic to us so we have become at odds with the world. To change this dangerous situation, we should realize our hatred is in our mind. We have to get rid of it so we can perceive the world as it really is.

We either project our thoughts outward or extend our love outward. Therefor, we must look inward before we look out. First we must look in and choose the guide we want to use for seeing – either the Holy Spirit or the ego. Then we will look out and view in the world what we want in ourselves, because we put it there. So we will find what we seek. If we see what we do not want, we are still projecting what we do want because we have accepted two different goals. The mind thinks it sees a divided world outside itself, but not within. This gives it the illusion it is whole, pursuing one goal. But we cannot be healed as long as we perceive the world as split. If we learn to pursue only one goal then we will be healed.

The only goal we should pursue is love. Then we will see nothing else. When we see other results, it is because we have looked in our mind and accepted opposition to love there. We looked for it there but we do not believe it is true. It reflects only our decision about reality. If we make love our only goal, it will come to us because we invited it. If we are afraid of love then we will not see it.

This world is a world of separation. We have no control over it because it is not a world that obeys God's Will. It is governed by the desire to be not like God. It is totally chaotic, governed by senseless "laws" and without any kind of meaning. It is made of what we do not want and are afraid of. It is in its maker's mind only. However, our salvation is also here. When we realize where the world is we will gain control over it because we do have control over our own mind.

All attack that we perceive is in our mind. The altar of God is there also. Christ lives there and has placed the Atonement on the altar for us. If we bring our perceptions there then we will see our vision changed as we learn to see truly. To find this place, we must give up all investment in the world. From this place the Holy Spirit will extend the real world to us. God and His Son live in peace here and we are forever welcome.

The Son of God cannot be driven by events that are outside of him. Any happenings that come to him are his choice, coming from within his mind. In every situation his power of decision is in control. No accident or chance is possible within the universe as God created it. And there is nothing outside it. If we suffer, then we have decided sin was our goal. If we are happy, then we gave the power of decision to the Holy Spirit. This is the little gift we offer to Him. He gives this to us to give to ourselves. By this gift we are given the power to release our savior, so he can give us salvation.

Unity Through Christ

Faith can move mountains. It is a power so great it can keep the Son of God in chains simply because he *believes* he is in chains. He can be released from them by simply withdrawing faith that they can hold him, and placing it in his freedom instead. Faith can be placed one way only. If it is given to sin then it is withdrawn from holiness – place it in holiness and it is taken away from sin.

Faith, belief and vision are all means. The Holy Spirit uses them to lead us on the path to the goal of holiness, the real world, away from all illusions. He sees this one direction only. He will remind us when we wander off the path. It is what we call a guilty conscious, the little nagging voice in our inner ear. When we have accepted His faith, belief and vision as our own, we will no longer need them. Heaven is reached through them, but once the state of certainty is reached, they are no longer meaningful.

In our private world we react to love as if it were fear and to fear as if it were love. We are drawn to fear and populate our world with figures of fear. Love repels us so we do not see all the love our brothers offer us. We are blind to the hand reaching out for our own, avoiding our brother's offering..

Our holy relationship, reborn and blessed in every holy instant, is the means by which thousands will rise to Heaven with us. We cannot plan for or prepare ourselves for such a function. But God wills it, so it is possible. He will not change

His Mind about it. By entering into a holy relationship we have accepted His purpose for this, and He will provide the means to anyone who shares His purpose.

A holy relationship cannot achieve its purpose when sin is used as the means to try to achieve its end. Those who love cannot judge. When we see a body we are using judgement, which we taught ourselves. We see it because we lack vision, which we can learn from the Holy Spirit. His vision cannot look upon sin so He cannot see the body. Our holy brother is not an illusion. If we try to see him in darkness then our evil imaginings will seem real there and we see him as a body. Our purpose was to shut him out so we closed our eyes. This seeing with closed eyes seems to be worth our effort as long as we believe in our purpose. Therefor, we will not see him as he really is.

We should not ask how we can see our brother without a body. Instead, we should ask if we really wish to see him as sinless. We should remember that when we see his sinlessness we will escape from fear. The Holy Spirit's goal is salvation, which will be achieved using vision when love has replaced all fear.

When we look on our brother's sinlessness with the Holy Spirit's vision, peace will come to us. Peace comes to all those who ask for it with real desire and who share the Holy Spirit's purpose. If we are willing to see our brother as sinless then we are in harmony with the Holy Spirit on what salvation is. Christ will rise before our vision, giving us great joy. Let us place no value on our brother's body for he wants to see himself as sinless as we do. Instead, let us bless the Son of God in our relationship.

What if we looked within and saw no sin there? If we ask this question we threaten the ego's whole defense system. It can no longer pretend to be our friend. Those who have joined in a holy relationship no longer believe their identity lies in the ego. Our belief in sin already has been shaken. We are now willing to look within and not see any sin, only mistakes we have made.

The ability to communicate mind to mind instead of to separate is reborn in each holy relationship. A holy relationship is like a baby in its rebirth. In this infant our vision is returned to us. He speaks the language we both understand. No two brothers can unite except through Christ. This child has been given to us to teach what we do not understand. He could never find a home in separate ones. He depends on the holiness of our relationship to let Him live.

God entrusted His Son to the worthy. Those who joined must have had communication restored to them, because they could not have joined through bodies. Reason will tell us that they must have seen each other through a vision that is not of the body. They must have communicated in a language that is not of the body. Each must have seen in the other a shelter where his Self could be reborn in safety and in peace.

To abide with Christ here all we need do is share His vision. His vision is given to anyone who is willing to see his brother as sinless. This willingness will be ours when we want to be entirely released from all effects of sin. We cannot reach Heaven while a single sin tempts us to remain here in distress. Heaven is the home of perfect purity. God created it for us. Our holy brother, sinless as ourselves, will lead us there.

Our Brother is Our Savior

There are two sons. They both appear to walk this earth without ever meeting. Our own beloved son we perceive as being outside ourselves. The other, the Father's Son, rests within both ourselves and our brother. Their differences are not in appearance or what they do. They have different purposes. This is what joins them to their counterpart. It separates them from all parts with a different purpose. The Son of God keeps his Father's Will. The son of man perceives an alien will and thinks he sees his wishes in it. His perception answers his wish by making it appear to be true. But perception can serve another goal. It is not bound by specialness but by choice. We can use perception for a different purpose. What we will see will serve that purpose. It will prove its own reality to us.

There are only two lessons to be learned. The lesson that God's Son is guilty produces the world we see. It is a world of terror and despair. But our learning can produce another outcome. No matter how much we over-learned our chosen task, the lesson that reflects God's Love is stronger. We will learn God's Son is innocent and we will see another world.

We cannot enter Heaven if we still have even one illusion. A savior cannot be a judge, mercy cannot condemn and vision cannot damn, only bless. Whose function it is to save, will save. How he does it is beyond our understanding. When he does it is our choice. We made time and we can command it. We are not slaves to time or to the world we made.

We are all asleep and do not see all the loveliness surrounding us. We do not hear freedom calling to us to wake from our dream of death. Lost in our dreams of specialness, we hate the call that would wake us. We curse God because He did not make a reality out of our dream as we wished. But we curse God and die in dreams only. If we open our eyes we will see the savior God gave us – our brother standing beside us. We should look on him and give him back his birthright, which is also ours.

God calls to us from our savior. He asks that we join His Will to save both our brother and ourselves from hell. Look on the print of nails on our brother's hands, held out to us for our forgiveness. God asks our mercy on His Son and on Himself. Let us not deny them. They are asking only that our will be done. They seek our love that we may love ourselves. We must not love our specialness instead of Them. The print of nails is on our hands also. We should forgive our Father, it was not His Will that we be crucified.

Our role in the universe is to be assigned the salvation from the misery of hell of the holy ones entrusted to us. We learn this when we first look on a brother as we look on ourselves and see the mirror of ourselves there. The concept of the evil little self is laid aside. Nothing will stand between our sight and what we look on. We will see the face of Christ in this single vision. The veil is lifted and light is there where darkness was before.

The Little Space

The veil across the face of Christ, the fear of God and of salvation, and the love of guilt and death are all different forms of the same error. We think there is a space between us and our brother, keeping us apart by an illusion of ourselves that keeps him at a distance from us. We give the sword of judgement to the illusion of ourselves so it may fight to keep this space empty of love. We invented a little gap between illusions and the truth where we think our safety lies. Our Self is hidden there by what we made. While we hold the sword we are assured of being separate from the one who holds the mirror of what we are, waiting to join us in love.

To be the savior of the Son of God we have to give up the wish to stay here in hell. First, we must look within and expect to see only innocence there. Holiness is seen through holy eyes that expect to see innocence everywhere they look. They call it forth from everyone they look upon, and our brother will be what they expect him to be. The savior sees his innocence in all he looks on, he sees his salvation everywhere. He brings the light to what he sees.

The savior's vision looks with innocence on what our brother is. He is free of any judgement made in the past because he sees no past in anyone. He has a wholly open mind, unclouded by past concepts and is prepared to look only on what the present holds. He cannot judge because he knows he does not have the knowledge. He asks for the meaning of what he sees and the answer is given to him. The door is held open for the face of Christ to shine on him.

When we are willing to give everything we held outside of truth to the Holy Spirit, He will take it from us. We do not do this, He does. If we lose our peace of mind because a brother is using fantasy to try to solve his problems, it is because we are not forgiving ourselves for supporting his fantasies. Therefor, both of us are kept from truth and salvation. Let us forgive him and we will restore to truth what we both denied to it.

Both were created together as one by a loving Father. When we see what "proves" otherwise, we are denying our reality. The instant of release will come to us when we admit that everything standing between us and keeping us separate from each other and our Father was made by us in secret. Its effects will be gone because its source will be uncovered. Its seeming independence from its source keeps us prisoner. It is the same mistake as thinking we are independent of our Source.

Christ's vision is given to anyone who is willing to see his brother as sinless. When we want to be entirely released from all effects of sin then we will be willing to see only sinlessness in our brother. We cannot reach Heaven while a single sin tempts us to remain here in hell. Heaven is the home of perfect purity. God created it for us. Our holy brother, who is as sinless as we are, will lead us there.

We are united in God's Will, we are the same as God Himself. We have one purpose which He gave to both of us. As we join in will, His Will is brought together. We are made complete by offering completion to our brother. Let us give him honor and not see the sinfulness that he sees. The power of salvation has been given to both of us and only waits for our choice. We can escape from darkness into light together. We can see as one, what was never separate or apart from all of God's Love.

We will not share evil dreams if we forgive the dreamer and perceive he is not the dream he made. Therefor, he cannot be part of our dream, from which we both are free. When we share an evil dream, it is because we believe we are that dream. We fear it and do not want to know our own Identity, thinking It is fearful. We make war on and deny our Self, believing we are an illusion. There is no compromise, we believe we are either an illusion or our Self.

Everyone will find release in his own way and in his own time. A holy relationship is a means of saving time. Time is saved because we are together with our brother. The universe is restored to both in one instant. We can save time by practicing the holy instant. All we need do is say to ourselves, "I need do nothing" and experience only the present instant. If we believe it for only an instant we will achieve more than a hundred years of contemplation or struggle against temptation.

By recognizing that we need do nothing, we diminish the body's value to nothing in our mind. This is the key to open a door through which we can slip past centuries of effort and escape from time. Sin will immediately lose all attraction. Time is denied when we do nothing, the past and future are gone. We have made a place within where the body ceases to demand attention. Thc Holy Spirit will come and stay in this place. He will stay there even when we forget and let the body's activity occupy our conscious mind. We will always be able to return to this place of rest. The body is not there in this quiet center. We will be directed on how to use the body sinlessly from here.

Every situation can be an opportunity to heal the Son of God. All we need do is offer our faith to him, giving him to the Holy Spirit. Let us release him from the demands our egos make of him and then we will properly perceive him as free. The Holy Spirit shares in this vision so He heals through us. We are joined in a united purpose. We came without the body, joining with the mind, where all healing is, so the body is healed.

The memory of God and of our ancient home in Heaven lies in everyone. There is an ancient song that we know and can hear if we listen. It is a song of praise to our Creator. Our self-made blindness cannot stand before this song. The remembering is a miracle. The light in one awakens it in all. When we see it in our brother, we will remember for everyone.

ing is a miracle. The light in one awakens it in all. When we see it in our brother, we will remember for everyone.

The body was made to be a sacrifice to sin. It is seen as sinful in the darkness. But in vision's light it is looked on differently. We can place our faith in it to serve the Holy Spirit's goal. This will give it power to be the means to help the blind to see. They will look past it, and so will we. We have given faith and belief from our mind to our body. We must give them back so the mind can use them to save itself from what it made.

Our task is to not let the form of our brother's mistakes keep us from him. We must not let what the body's eyes see keep the vision of his holiness from us. We must not let the perception of his sins and body block our awareness of him. We believe we can attack him because we associate sin with his body. His holiness and our salvation are beyond his errors. We have tried to see our sins in him to save ourselves. His holiness will show us our forgiveness. We cannot be saved by making sinful the one whose holiness is our salvation.

We can have freedom of either the mind or the body, but not of both. If we see either one of them as means, then the other is seen as the end. Means serve the end. As the end is reached, the value of the means decreases. Everyone is seeking for freedom where he believes it is. He believes either the mind or the body will achieve it. Whichever he chooses, he will make the other his choice as the means to find it.

If we choose that the body be free then the mind will be used as means. The mind's value is its ability to contrive ways to achieve the body's freedom. But freedom of the body is meaningless. The mind is dedicated to serving illusions. No one has any idea of what is valuable in this confusing situation. But the Holy Spirit waits in gentle patience, as sure of the outcome as He is of His Creator's Love. He knows this mad decision was made by one as dear to His Creator as love is to itself.

We can temporarily protect the body a little. What we think we save, we hurt. Both its health and its harm lie in the choice we save it for. If we choose to save it for show, or as bait to catch another, or to house specialness in better style, or to weave a frame of loveliness around our hate, then we condemn it to decay and death. If we see any of these purposes in our brother's body, then we are condemning our own. If we weave a frame of holiness around him then the truth will shine on us and keep us safe from decay.

We will scc what we believe and we can change what we believe. The body can only follow, never lead. We can release our body from imprisonment. We should never want to hold our chosen enemies in guilt. We should not want to keep our chosen friends in chains to the illusion of a changing love. Love is as changeless as the Father's Love for all. And to feel God's Love within is to see a bright and beautiful world filled with light where we are safe from every form of danger and pain

"We read that we ought to forgive our enemies, but we do not read that we ought to forgive our friends."

Sir Francis Bacon

Chapter 10

THE LIGHT WITHIN

Introduction

We are all entitled to miracles. When miracles do not happen, something has gone wrong. Miracles show we are filled with light, we are loving and we are lovable. Our inner peace is the peace of God and cannot be denied by anything external to us. We can deny the cause of errors, or darkness, by shining the light within us on them. There is a spark that can grow into radiance so that the mind will be filled with light and will bring the body into harmony with itself when it realizes it is the learner, not the body.

As long as we believe we are in a separated state we need prayer. Our natural state is communion, because we are inseparable from God. We are the Thoughts of God and we live in His Light. It is impossible for us to perceive our own worth in the ego's world. But when we learn to know ourselves in the One Light then the miracle that we are will become perfectly clear to us.

Let Our Brother's Light Shine

Our mind can make the belief in separation very real and, because of the power of the mind, the belief is very powerful. We call this belief the "devil." It is powerful, active and destructive. It is in direct opposition to God because it denies His Fatherhood. What the devil has made of our life will vanish when it is exposed to the light of truth because its foundation is a lie. Our true foundation is our creation by God. It cannot be shaken because the light is in it. We started as truth and we are trying to return to our Beginning. As we approach the Beginning, we will find our Self there still in peace. But we are afraid to go back because we believe our thought system will be destroyed. What will actually happen is our thought system will be corrected by the light from the true Foundation of life.

We all have an inner light of joy. Unfortunately we inhibit our own happiness because we are afraid of our feelings. There are many opportunities to gladden ourselves but we usually refuse, preferring to be sorrowful instead. Joy attracts a willingness to share it, encouraging the mind's natural impulse to respond as one with the Sonship. Every joyful thought by any brother anywhere blesses us because the light is so strong it radiates throughout the Sonship and returns thanks to God Himself. A Child of God can only love his brother as he loves himself.

The same Mind that decided for our elder brother is in each of us. We can let it change our thinking because it hears only one Voice. We are the light of the world along with our elder brother. Our task is to waken the world to the Call for God. Everyone will answer the Call of the Holy Spirit or the Sonship cannot be one. Our part is to teach our brother as we learn.

The Holy Spirit reinterprets what the ego makes by using His understanding, because He understands the Laws of God. Understanding is light. The Holy Spirit reinterprets us as the light of the world, as God created us to be. He acts on behalf of God.

We make our world by projecting the images in our mind. God creates by extending Himself. God's thought system is light. We are the cornerstone of it. As we approach the center of it the clearer the light of the Great Rays becomes. As we approach the center of the ego's thought system, the darker and more obscure the way becomes. The little spark in our mind is enough to illuminate the foundation of the ego's thought system and expose its weakness. If we judge it honestly in the light, we will see it rests on nothingness. Everything we have been afraid of is based on a foundation of nothing.

The journey through this world is one of pain, fear and grief. This dark path is not the way God Wills for His Son. Let us learn to walk in the light instead. It is not a hard way but it is very different than the one we now follow. If we remember that the Great Light surrounds us always and is shining out from us, we will prevail. We cannot see the dark companions we have made when the light shines on them. Deny them instead of denying the light. The way will be clear then.

It is impossible to hide the glory God gave us. It is His Will that we be glorious and use the power He gave us to create. He gave us the light shining in us. When we stray we are wandering on a journey of illusions in conflict. God will lead us to the light when we show our willingness to follow. If we turn toward the light, the little spark in us is part of a Light so great that it will carry us out of all darkness forever. To make the way easier, God placed a Guide in our mind. We must turn to Him and ask Him the way back to the Father and our home in Heaven.

The dark, would-be comforters have no place in God's temple. We should never let them enter the mind of God's Son. The children of light cannot live in darkness. When tempted to deny Him, let us remember there are no other gods to place before Him and accept His Will in peace. When we fear salvation, we are choosing death, darkness and perception instead of life, light and knowledge. If we believe these can be reconciled then we believe God and His Son can not. Our kingdom was given to us from beyond this world.

Our peace is limitless because we share it with all our brothers. If we try to limit it then we will not know our Self. Every altar to God is part of everyone. The light He created is one. When we cut off a brother from our light, we are darkening our own mind. The way back is to bring him back with us so we can enter the light together. That is God's law. It protects the wholeness of His Son.

We are the only ones who can deprive ourselves of anything. When we understand this and place our belief in it, this realization will lead us to the light. It is crucial to our reawakening. We must oppose any denial of this fact. In the early stages of a holy relationship we may withdraw blame from external happenings and place it within. This can be very painful because we do not realize there is no difference between what is within us and what is without.

To heal ourselves, we must love ourselves. If we do not, we are denying ourselves the love that would heal. The miracle worker translates denial into truth. To be healed, we have to let the light, which we have blocked in another mind, shine into our own. The light will shine brightly despite the heavy, dark fog surrounding it. If we give no power to the fog the light will shine through. Let us remember that all power is of God. Let us remember this for our brother, for God cannot be remembered alone. And we will be remembering for all the Sonship because each mind contains all minds.

The Vision of Christ

When we learn the cost of sleeping, we will decide to wake. We will see the real world and then we will remember the Father, the Son and the Holy Spirit. Christ is waiting to be seen and wants to share the real world with us. He waits in perfect peace at His Father's altar. He holds out His Father's Love to us in the quiet light of the Holy Spirit's blessing. The Holy Spirit will lead everyone home to the Father. Christ is waiting there as His Self, the Son of God.

Let us deny the separation so we can have knowledge reinstated to us. All the problems we think we face in this world are only aspects of the one basic problem – the separation. There seems to be a constant stream of problems that need solutions. We never seem to be able to solve them all and so we become discouraged. The way to solve all problems is simple – we have to find our way back to God. Then there will be no more problems – only light, joy and happiness, our natural state of being.

When we approach the altar of God within, our perception of God's Son will become so enlightened that light will come streaming in to our awareness. The spirit of God's Son will shine in the Mind of God and become one with Him. God shines on Himself loving His Son, the extension of Himself. Let us bring all our suffering and pain to His Light that it may be healed. He will take every little hurtful thought and purify it, restoring it to His magnitude. If we bring all our guilty little secrets to the light, the Light will eliminate them. Then we will remember our Father.

In our private world we are sleeping. We see in darkness what we made. Our eyes are closed yet we see because we have denied vision. This denial means we accept insanity. We believe we can make a private world in which we decide what we see. To have vision we must let the darkness go. If we let the light shine on our dreams they will disappear, for vision needs light. Vision cannot come through our eyes. They were made to see in darkness. Beyond this and within us is the vision of Christ Who looks on all in light.

Christ is revealed in the Holy Spirit's Light. All who ask for light will see Christ. They will not be alone because He is no more alone than they are. Seeing the Son within, they will rise to the Father because they recognized the Christ and understood. Looking upon themselves with love, they will see themselves as the Holy Spirit sees them. All the beauty of the sane world will shine on them.

Using past experience to judge the present is unnatural. The past we remember is based on illusions. We must learn to look upon everyone without referring to his or our own past and we will learn from what we see *now*. If we are afraid of light the past will cast a dark cloud over the present, concealing our brother's identity from us. We cannot hear the Holy Spirit's Voice within us when we keep grievances from the past and use them to judge the present.

If we hold the past against our brothers we are choosing to remain in darkness. In the present the light that would free us from the past is offered to us. The present is the one changeless dimension of time. We can look there at Christ and call upon Him to shine on us. He will not deny the truth in us because we looked for it in Him and found it.

Salvation lies in the *now* of time. Let us reach out to our brothers with the touch of Christ. Our continuity in eternity is shared with them in timeless union. We will see the light within when we shine our light on our brothers. Let us call all our brothers to see the light in us. Everyone has his part in giving thanks for the light to the Creator. If we give love to the sick they will shine on us with holy thanks. They will guide us to the joy and peace we gave them

In this world we can give a light that is not of it. This light will attract us to follow it and find another world. We will lay aside this world and find the other, real world bright with the love we gave it. We will shine in gratitude with unlimited light on all those we brought with us because they brought us here. Our light will join with theirs in such compelling power all the others will be drawn out of their darkness.

All the senseless things the ego urges us to get will be taken from us and thrown into the dust when we are saved. We will lose whatever we got in the ego's name. We should not ask ourselves what we need. We do not know. Our advice to ourselves would only hurt us. What we think we need would darken our world against the light. We would not want to question the value of this world. We should ask the Holy Spirit what we need.

Spreading Peace Through the Sonship

The Holy Spirit knows what we need. He will give us everything we ask for that does not block the light. He knows all our needs are temporary. They will last until we step aside and realize they are all fulfilled. He has no interest in what He gives us except to make certain we will not use them to linger in time. He does not want to delay our homecoming.

Let us leave all our needs to Him for what He supplies is safe for us. He will guide us on a journey that we will travel with a light heart. His sight is fixed on the journey's end. His goal is within God's Son. Within himself God's Son has no needs. Regardless of how holy his perception becomes, his inheritance is not outside himself. The light in him needs only to shine in peace, letting the rays extend in quiet to infinity.

When temptation tries to lead us on a useless journey away from light, let us remember what we really want, and say: "I would follow the Holy Spirit Who leads me to Christ." Then let us follow Him joyously through all dangers in this world. Let us have faith that He will lead us in complete safety. We should not seek for things we will lose. We should be content with what we will surely keep in our quiet journey to peace.

This is how salvation is achieved: When we meet a brother, say to him,

> "My peace I give to you in glad exchange for all the sorrow the world has offered you. Together we will spread peace across the world's sad face like a ray of light."

And we will see the joyous beauty spread from face to face as peace is spread throughout the Sonship.

Every aspect of creation *is* the whole. When we offer a miracle to the Son of God our perception becomes one aspect of the miracle of creation. We must see everyone without their past, only their beauty *now*. This will bring us nearer the end of time by bringing light into the darkness. Then Christ's vision will be possible. Let us help Him give His gift of light to everyone in the darkness.

When we see our brother is the same as ourselves we will be released from prison and gain knowledge. When we answer our elder brother's call and unite with him we will grow in strength and no one will remain untouched. Time will be over. The holy light we saw will be returned to us.

Guilt hides the Father because guilt is an attack on God's Son. The guilty condemn, linking the future to the past, for this is the ego's law. We cannot awaken from the darkness while we obey the ego's laws. They do not let the light in because violations are severely punished. We believe we are guilty and must condemn when we follow the ego's laws. But if we let God's laws of Atonement intervene between past and future then the light will shine so brightly the darkness will disappear.

The ego tells us not to look within because of the guilt we will find there. What it is trying to conceal from us is the light placed there by God. Let us resolve to look within because we will find that what we were afraid to find has been replaced with love. Our elder brother will teach us how to relinquish the ego to the light of spirit, by teaching us how its thought system arose. The ego will be frightened by this.

The ego is undone when it is brought to God. It is undone because by bringing error to truth, the contradiction cannot stand. It disappears in light. It is not attacked, it simply vanishes. Reality cannot change with time or mood or chance. It cannot be undone or changed because it is real and changeless.

We have forgotten how much our Father loves us and how much we love Him. We show no mercy to ourselves or to our brothers because of this. Let us look past the cloud of guilt, dimming our vision to the lovely truth shining within us. Christ would have us see the altar to our Father in the holy place where the light shines. Nothing can keep us from seeing the altar. It is as pure as He Who raised it to Himself. Christ offers mercy to all God's children, and He wants us to offer mercy to everyone also.

The only way to look within and see the light of love is to release our brothers from the guilt we have projected on them. We who have always loved the Father can never be afraid to look within because we will find no guilt, only love. The Holy Spirit will restore reason to us by removing all illusions when we show Him our little willingness. Reason will tell us that our guilt is not reasonable. It is not in the Mind of God where we are. The Holy Spirit will show us the perfect purity shining in us through Christ's vision.

He will bring the light of truth into our darkness. Our brothers will see this light in us and realize we did not make it. The sight of it will teach them release from the darkness of the ego's works. The heavy chains binding them to despair will disappear under the light, for they are nothing and are easily shined away. We will see this with them. They will teach us release and gladness because that is what we have taught them.

The Holy Spirit's plan is to free us from the past. He wants us to be happy. The happy learner will meet the conditions of learning in this world. The simple lesson, truth is true, holds the key to the dark door we believe is locked forever. Light is the key to the door and is within all of us. Let us accept it from Christ's hands. Let us join Him in the holy task of bringing the light to all. The light He holds out to us will free us and our brothers from our sleep of darkness. But we are not aware of this because our guilt hides it.

When we see our brothers as free, without a body, we will be free of darkness. As we wake them with our light, so will they wake us. The instant we perceive Christ's vision, we give it. We will realize it is impossible to deny the simple truth when everything becomes clear. There is nothing else, for God is everywhere. His Son is in Him and everything is his.

We are the only one who can ask a penalty of ourselves. Every moment with a brother is a chance to offer healing, love and light. If we refuse then we bind ourselves to darkness because we did not choose to free him and enter the light with him. We chose to be afraid of both darkness and light. But we can learn that nothingness has no power over us. The Holy Spirit teaches the happy lesson that darkness has no power over God's Son. It is His joy to teach this. It will be our joy to teach with Him as we learn.

If we try to steal the Son of God's inheritance – the Kingdom – we will feel guilty. We must protect his purity by bringing our innocence to the light. Let us shine away the veils of guilt behind which he hides. When we will bring the light of guiltlessness to guilt then guilt will be shined away. We should not keep them apart for we cannot have them both. Only one means anything, the other is wholly without sense.

The Holy Spirit lives within us in the light of perfect openness, patiently waiting for us to listen to His lessons. Nothing is hidden so nothing He teaches is fearful. The light of love will dispel all darkness except what we have kept apart from love. The darkness has sentinels, (illusions) made out of nothing, guarding our access to the Holy Spirit. We made them as part of our childish game and now we are afraid of them. We should not be afraid of these strange ideas of safety. They are nothing. Let us let them go and we will find that what was fearful will be gone. Only the light of love will remain.

The Holy Spirit will remove whatever interferes with communication. Let us bring our dark sentinels to Him. He will not attack them but will teach us that in the light, they are not to be dreaded. Let us open all dark doors and let the light come streaming in. God's temple has no hidden chambers. Its gates are open wide. His Son is welcome there. Everyone will come to where God has called him, unless he closes the door himself.

The Mirror of the Mind

We can have either light (knowledge) or darkness (ignorance), but not both. If we bring opposites together then everything that is not real will disappear. Light will dispel darkness as knowledge will dispel ignorance. Perception, with all deceit removed, brings ignorance to knowledge.

When we will not let our belief in darkness go, light cannot enter our mind. Truth does not do battle with ignorance. Love does not attack fear. Truth and love do not need protect-ion. We made all these defenses we have put between ourselves and our brothers. God does not know of them. Everything we made will be gently turned to our good by the Holy Spirit. He perceives our defenses as a call for what we have attacked with them. We should not be concerned with how the Holy Spirit can perform this mighty task. The power of God is with Him. All we are asked to do is the little He suggests to us. We merely have to trust Him and we will see how easy these tasks are.

The Holy Spirit will gladly enter our consciousness and shine away our fears. He will look upon everything we bring to Him and dispel the dark shadows that have frightened us. But if we conceal anything from Him, then He cannot help us. The vision of Christ is for Him and for us. When we both look upon the light He holds and the darkness we hold, they cannot coexist. If we join our perception to His then His judgement will triumph.

We should not let our mind wander from the light's center into darkened side corridors. If we choose to go astray, the Guide appointed for us can bring us back to where God and His Son wait for our recognition. Together they will give us the gift of oneness which will dispel all separation. We have to realize the glory of God and His Son belong to us. Let us return and unite with them, for we can join only with reality.

We can be a mirror reflecting the holiness of our Creator. The light of Heaven can shine from us to all those around us. We must not let the images of other gods (the ego's world) dim the mirror. God Himself will shine upon it when we leave the mirror clean and clear of all darkened images. Only He can be perceived in it.

From a clean mirror, reflections seen in light are clear. But any darkness dims the message that is reflected so it becomes open to interpretation. If we clean our mirror then all our brothers will understand the message we are sending out. It comes from the Holy Spirit in us, Who holds it out to the mirror in our brother. He will recognize it because he has been taught his need for it. He does not know where to look, so let him see it in us and we will share it with him.

All the healing power of God Himself can be brought to the world through the reflection of God shining in us. We should wait no longer to clean the mirror of our mind to receive the image of holiness. Those who will look upon it will understand its meaning. Everyone whose problems are brought to the light will be healed.

Although our thoughts may conflict, they can occur concurrently and in great numbers. In this world of separation we classify some of them as more important, larger or smaller, better or worse, wiser or more stupid, etc., than others. Some thoughts are reflections of Heaven. Others are motivated by the ego, which only seems to think.

This results in a constantly changing pattern shifting across the mirror of our mind. The reflection of Heaven lasts for only a moment as the darkness blots out the light. Light and darkness are constantly sweeping across our mind. We establish a sense of order that holds the little sanity remaining to us. This shows we are not an ego for the ego's world is complete chaos. The order we impose limits the ego. But it also limits us because we are arranging things by using judgement when we install a system of order.

The Holy Spirit will teach us how to order our thoughts by giving us shining examples of miracles. Every call for help is answered in exactly the same way by the miracle. It does not judge which call is louder or greater or more important. We do not have to use our own judgement for the power of God is behind every miracle. It is proof we have the power of God in us. That is why the miracle gives equal blessing to all who share in it, and everyone shares in it. God's power, being limitless, offers everything to every call for help from anyone.

God cannot be remembered in secret and alone. To remember Him, we should let the Holy Spirit order our thoughts and give us the answer. Everyone is seeking for love. They are not aware of this unless they join with us in the search. When we seek for love together we possess a powerful light that gives meaning to what we see. When we seek alone we will fail.

What we have learned in this world has no meaning. Therefor, the present has no meaning for us, and we do not know how to undo the past. Everything in our past is what we taught ourselves and we are poor teachers. We must learn to let all the past go. Let us not attempt to understand *anything* in the present in its "light." If we do, we are trying to see in the darkness. We cannot illuminate our understanding using darkness. This contradicts the light.

God has another lesson for us. The Holy Spirit has learned this lesson for every child of light: *God's Happiness belongs to all of us.* He wants us to have it. To learn this lesson, we must be willing to bring all our dark lessons to truth. The Holy Spirit will gladly exchange them for the lesson He has learned for us.

Every problem we have can be solved by a miracle the Holy Spirit will offer to us. Every trial or fear or pain has been brought to light by Him and undone. Miracles are for us, only waiting for us to claim them. He has shined away all dark lessons with light, recognizing they never were. Lessons we want to teach ourselves do not exist in His mind. He has corrected them. He does not see the past. Every miracle He offers us corrects our use of time.

We must recognize the sick attraction for guilt for what it is. We must remove our investment in it and learn to let it go. We have not looked at what our attraction to guilt is. As we bring it to the light, we will start to wonder why we ever wanted it. If we look open-eyed we will see ugliness that does not belong in the holy mind of the host of God.

Heaven in the Holy Relationship

Let us see the star of Christmas as a light shining in the Heaven within us. We can accept it as a sign the time of Christ has come. He comes demanding no sacrifice of anyone. He is Host to God. Sacrifice means nothing in His Presence. Let us invite Him in by recognizing His Host is One. Love must be total to give Him welcome. The Host of God in the time of Christ cannot be touched by fear. The Host is as holy as the Perfect Innocence He protects, and Whose power protects Him.

As we cross the bridge from the real world to our home in Heaven, we will gain the understanding of where Heaven is. It will join with and become one with us. Each light that returns to Heaven increases the joy. We should wait no longer for the Love of God. Let us let the holy instant come to us and speed us on our way.

We are faithless to our brother because we blame him for what we did to him. It is our own past we hold against him. We lack faith in him because of what we were. But the past never was so we are as innocent of what we were as he is. Therefor, there is no cause for faithlessness.

There *is* Cause for faith. Where Its purpose is shared, that Cause enters the situation. The light of truth shines from the center of the situation, touching everyone in it. Every situation involves our whole holy relationship. If we keep something of ourselves outside then it is no longer holy.

We both have been called to the most holy function in this world. It is offered us in our holy relationship. We should accept it and give it as we have accepted it. It reaches out to heal and comfort every broken fragment of the Sonship. The peace of God is given to us. The holy light that brought us together will extend to all the Sonship.

We have spent our life going from waking to sleeping, bringing truth to illusion and reality to dreams. We have gone on and on, always into deeper sleep. Every fantasy that seemed to bring light only made the darkness deeper. We sought a blackness so complete we could hide from truth forever, completely insane. We forgot God cannot destroy Himself and we are part of God. The dark clouds can cover the light in us but cannot put it out.

When the light starts to come nearer, we hasten off to the "security" of darkness, retreating to fear. We shrink from the truth because we fear the unknown. But we will advance because our goal is to move from fear to truth. You have indicated your willingness to accept the goal of knowledge by reading this book. When we falter and have stepped back in fear into the darkness, let us join with our elder brother in an instant of light . He will remind us that our goal is light.

When we joined hands with our brother we were not alone. We hold our elder brother's hand also, he is always in a holy relationship. This world's light is in our holy relationship. Let us not be tempted to take away the gift of faith we gave our brother. The gift is given forever. God Himself receives it. We have accepted God so we cannot take it back. We do not understand yet what we accepted but our understanding is not necessary. The *wish* to understand was all that was necessary. It was the desire to be holy. The Will of God is granted us because we desire the only thing we ever had or ever were.

The Son of God hid in the darkness. But we bring Heaven to him in our holy relationship. We have joined with our elder brother in this. Our willingness to bring darkness to light gives strength to all those who would remain in the darkness. The light will come to those who seek it. They will join with our elder brother and carry it into the darkness. He needs us as we need him for salvation. We answered his call when we joined our brother.

From within our holy relationship we bring salvation. Now we have the function of bringing light to the darkness. Let us carry the light from the holy instant back to the darkness. We should not worry about time. Our fear is in the past. Time has been readjusted to help us do, together with our elder brother, what we could not do separately. Love will always join two minds which have joined in the desire for love.

Every light in Heaven goes with us. Every ray that shines forever in God's Mind shines on us. They give the little spark of our desire the power of God Himself. We are coming home with our brother after a long and meaningless journey we each took separately, leading nowhere. We light each other's way. The Great Rays extend from this light back into darkness and forward into God. They shine away the past to make room for His eternal Presence, in Which everything is radiant in the light.

Returning Home at Easter

The Holy Spirit has brought union to us. He has returned our little offering of darkness to the eternal light. The way this is done is extremely simple because of what this kingdom really is. The wasteland of this world is seen only through the body's eyes. The body's sight is distorted. It sends tiny little meaningless messages to us. The body is the proof that guilt is real as long as we believe in it. Its actions are dictated by guilt. We made this world to limit our awareness; we do this by restricting the magnitude of the messages we receive.

Guilt is an illusion that seems to be a heavy and impenetrable foundation for the ego's thought system. When we see the light shining behind it, its thinness will become apparent. We will see it as a fragile veil. It is like a bank of low dark clouds that seems to be a solid wall, hiding the sun. Its illusion of impenetrability will give way when we see the mountain tops rising above it. It has no power to stop anyone willing to climb above it and see the sun shining on the ego's dark foundation. It cannot stop the fall of a feather. If we try to grasp it we will be holding nothing.

In the cloud bank it is easy to see a whole world rising in our imagination. The proof of our senses assure us it is there. Figures move about and seem real. Forms shift from loveliness to the grotesque as long as we play the children's game of make believe. But we should never confuse the world of imagination with the world below or try to make it real.

It should be the same with the dark clouds of guilt. If we travel through them we will not be bruised. Our Guide will lead us past them. Beneath them is a world of light. Their shadows fall on the world beyond them but they cannot fall on the world of light. This brightness forms a shining circle that is the real world.

Forgiveness will release us but it is not the end of our journey. It makes lovely but it does not create. It is the source of healing. It is the messenger of love, but not its Source. We are led here so God can take the final step. A step still further inward that we cannot take. It transports us to the Source of light.

The Holy Spirit asks us to receive the gratitude we owe Him. If we look with gentle graciousness on our brother we will see Him. We cannot see the Holy Spirit. But we can see the light in our brothers. When the extension of the peace in us encompasses everyone, the Holy Spirit's function here will be accomplished. God will take the last step Himself. The Holy Spirit will gather all the thanks and gratitude we have offered Him. He will lay them before His Creator in the name of His most holy Son. The Father will accept them in His name. There will be no necessity for seeing in the presence of His gratitude.

Our home has been carefully prepared for us on the other side, beyond the veil. It has called to us since time began. We heard, but did not know where to look, or how. Now we do. The knowledge is in us, waiting to be freed from all the terror that kept it hidden. It is our Easter time. We will hear the glad song of Easter – the Son of God was never crucified. Let us lift up our eyes together in faith, not fear. In our vision the pathway to the door of Heaven will be open. We will share our home in quietness, gentleness and peace.

Our holy brother will lead us there. The guiding light of his innocence will light our way. It shines from the holy altar within him where we laid the lilies of our forgiveness. Let us go beyond the veil of fear, lighting each other's way. Let us find what we were meant to find by Him Who leads us. The holiness leading us is within, as is our home.

The Power of Love

Perfect love knows no fear because it knows no sin. It looks on others the same as it looks on itself. The innocent see only safety. The pure in heart see God within His Son. They look to the Son to lead them to the Father. We have it in us now to lead our brother to the Father. Let us see in him the light of God's promise of immortality. If we see him as sinless we will lose all fear.

The blind must imagine what the world really looks like. It is the same with us, for we do not see. We stumble and fall on obstacles we do not recognize. Doors we think are closed to us are really open, waiting to welcome us. It is foolish to try to judge what we could see instead. We do not have to imagine what the world is really like. We can be shown which doors are open. We can see which way leads to light and safety, and which leads to darkness. We do not have to guess. Vision will always show us where to go, but judgement will always give us false directions.

The body was made to be a sacrifice to sin. It is seen as sinful in the darkness. But in vision's light it is looked upon differently. We can place our faith in it to serve the Holy Spirit's goal. This will give it power to be the means to help the blind to see. If we give faith, belief and perception to the body from our mind, we will look beyond it and see other, separated bodies. If we let them be given back, the mind can use them to save itself from what it made.

Beyond the bodies we have interposed between us is the holy relationship, shining in the golden light that reaches it from the bright endless circle that extends forever. We stand with our brother in this holy place, before the veil of sin hanging between us. It hangs between us and the face of Christ. Let us raise it together. It is a thin drapery that separates us, not a solid block. Peace will reach us here. We have no concept of what it will be like after we have crossed. The love of Christ will light our faces. It will shine from them into the darkened world. He will return with us from this holy place, not leaving it. We will become His messengers, returning Him unto Himself.

We who walk with Him will see loveliness. We will look beautiful to each other. We will be happy together after our long and lonely journey. We will open the gates of Heaven to the sorrowful. Everyone who looks upon the face of Christ in us will rejoice. We will bring the light we saw beyond the veil to the tired eyes of those as weary now as we once were. They will be thankful to see us, offering Christ's forgiveness to remove their faith in sin.

The holy relationship, lovely in its innocence, mighty in strength, blazes with a light brighter than the sun. It is chosen by our Father as a means for His Own plan. Everything given to it will be used. It has the power to heal all pain, regardless of its form. Neither of us can serve alone. Healing lies only in our joint will. Here is our healing and it is here we will accept Atonement. In our healing, the Sonship is healed because our wills are joined.

The light *has* come to us. We do not recognize the light we bring yet, but we will remember. Can we deny for ourselves the vision we bring to others? We will not fail to recognize a gift we let be laid in Heaven through ourselves . When we put ourselves in the service of the Holy Spirit, it is service to ourselves . We are now His means so we must love what He loves. We will remember all that is eternal. Nothing in time can remain in minds that serve the timeless. No illusions can disturb the peace of a relationship that is now the means for peace.

The Holy Spirit's function is the extension of forgiveness. We should leave this to Him. Let us give to Him what can be extended. We must not keep to ourselves any dark secrets He cannot use. Let us offer Him the tiny gifts He can extend forever. He will make a potent force for peace of each one. He will join to it the power God gave Him, to make each gift of love a source of healing for all. Our little gifts of love to our brother light up the world. Let us look away from darkness and toward each other. Let the darkness be scattered by Him Who knows the light. He will lay it on each smile of faith we bless each other with.

The light joining us shines throughout the universe. It makes us one with our Creator because it joins us. In Him all creation is joined. Our holy relationship can teach the power of love, making all fear impossible. Let us not try to keep a little of the ego with this gift. It teaches us we cannot be separate, which is a denial of the ego. Let us let truth decide for us. Are we different or the same? It will teach us which is true.

We should not let littleness lead God's Son into temptation. Let us help him rise above it and perceive the light. We must not leave him frightened and alone in his temptation in this world. Our innocence will light the way to his. When we realize Heaven's glory shines on him we will no longer walk trembling, alone and afraid, in a fearful world.

We are One in God's Will

Everything around us is part of us. We will see the light of Heaven in it when we look lovingly on it. We will come to understand all that is given to us. The world will shine in our forgiveness. Everything we once thought of as sinful will be reinterpreted as part of Heaven. We will walk, clean and redeemed, through a world in need of the redemption our innocence imparts. Our salvation and freedom are here. But it must be complete if we want to recognize it.

The light of our relationship is like the Love of God. It cannot be extended to all creation because our forgiveness of our brother is not complete yet. Each form of attack and murder that still attracts us limits the healing and the miracles we have the power to extend to everyone. The Holy Spirit understands how to increase our little gifts, making them mighty. He understands how our holy relationship is raised above the battleground. Our part is to realize attack in any form is not our will. Our purpose now is to overlook the battleground.

When we are tempted to attack, let us remember we *can* see the battle from above. We experience a stab of pain, a twinge of guilt and a loss of peace. When they occur, let us choose a miracle instead of murder. God Himself and all the lights of Heaven will lean toward us. We have chosen to be where He would have us be. Illusions cannot attack the peace of God together with His Son.

Those who share their Father's purpose, and know it is theirs, want for nothing. There is never any sorrow. They are only aware of the light they love. Only love shines on them forever. It is their past, present and future, always the same, eternally complete and wholly shared. Their happiness can never change.

The body does not need healing. It is the mind that is sick as long as it believes it is a body. Christ sets forth His remedy here. He enfolds the body in the light of His purpose.

It is filled with the holiness that shines from Him. It carries Him in gentleness and love to heal the minds of those who do not know Him. This is the mission our brother has for us. We have the same mission for him.

We are the means to return to God. We are not separate nor have a life apart from His. His life is manifest in us who are His Sons. Each aspect of Himself is framed in holiness and purity. Its radiance shines through each body it looks on. It brushes all darkness into light by looking past it to the light. The veil is lifted and nothing hides the face of Christ. We stand with our brother before Him to draw aside the veil that seems to keep us apart and separate.

We are the same as God Himself is One. We are not divided in His Will. We have one purpose. He gave the same to us both. As we join in will, His Will is brought together. We are made complete by offering completion to our brother. We must not see the sinfulness he sees. Let us give him honor so we may appreciate ourselves and him. The power of salvation is given to both of us. We can escape from darkness into light. We can see as one what was never separate or apart from all of God's Love.

Walk Beyond the Darkness to the Light

Everyone here is in darkness, but no one is alone. Heaven's Help is within each of us, ready to lead us out of darkness into light, at any time we choose. When we make this choice, we will see every situation, that seemed to justify our anger, turn into an event which justifies our love. We will understand at last that the calls to war we heard before were really calls to peace. Where we gave attack before, now we will perceive another altar where we can give forgiveness. We will reinterpret all temptation as a chance to bring joy.

It cannot be a sin to perceive wrongly. Let us look on our brother's errors as a chance for us to see how the Helper given to us works in transforming our misery into peace. We will see the world He made instead of ours.

If we ask ourselves: What is justified? What do we want? We will find that these two questions are the same. When we see them as the same, we will have made the right choice. We will be released from the belief there are two ways of seeing. This world has much to offer to our peace of mind. If we change our mind about our brother we will find there are many chances to extend our forgiveness. This is its purpose to those who want to have peace and forgiveness enfold them and to enter the light.

Minds that know they are joined cannot feel guilt. They cannot attack so this makes them happy because they see they are safe. The innocence they see brings them joy. Everyone is seeking for what will bring him joy. If we think the pursuit of sin will bring us joy then we will use the body as the means to find joy, resulting in the inevitable disappointment. But if we believe our happiness lies in seeing our brother as sinless, then we have chosen the correct means for joy.

The basic law of perception is – we will delight in what we see because we see it so we can be delighted. We will see suffering and sin as long as we think they bring us joy. What we wish is either harmful or beneficial to us. We chose it as a means to bring us these results in our belief they would make us happy. This law applies even in Heaven. The Son of God creates to bring joy to himself. He shares His Father's purpose in his own creation so his joy might be increased, and God's with his.

We made a world that is not so, but we can take comfort in another world where there is peace. We can bring this world to all the weary hearts that look on sin and beat to its sad refrain. We can bring peace to them. A world can rise from us where they will rejoice because their hearts are glad. There is a vision in us that extends to all of them. It will cover them in gentleness and light. In this widening world of light the darkness they thought was there will be pushed away. It will become distant shadows, forgotten as the sun shines them to nothingness. Their "evil" thoughts, their "sinful" hopes, their dreams of guilt and revenge, and every wish to kill and die, will disappear before the sun we bring.

Surely this is something we would do for the Love of God and for ourselves. This is what it would do for us – our "evil" thoughts will seem to be remote. They will go farther off because the sun in us has risen to push them away from the light forever. We will stand in innocence and quiet in the sunlight, wholly unafraid. The rest we find will be extended. Our peace will never fall away leaving us homeless. Those who offer peace to everyone will find a home in Heaven the world cannot destroy. It is large enough to hold the world within its peace.

All of Heaven is in us. Every leaf that falls is given life in us. Each bird that ever sang will sing again in us. Every flower that ever bloomed has saved its perfume and loveliness for us. No goal can replace the Will of God and of His Son that Heaven be restored to him. It was created as his only home. Nothing was before or after it, no other place, state or time, nothing else in any form. We can bring this to all the world and all the mistaken thoughts that entered it. There is no better way to bring our own mistakes to truth than by our willingness to bring the light of Heaven with us as we walk beyond the world of darkness into light.

The wish to see calls down the grace of God upon our eyes. It brings the gift of light that makes sight possible. If we want to see our brother correctly then God wills we recognize him as our savior. He wills that he keep the function He gave him. Do not let him remain lonely. The lonely see no function in the world for them to fulfill. They do not feel needed. They seem to have no aim which only they can perfectly fulfill.

We Stand on Holy Ground

We all have a special value here. We wanted it and it was given to us. The Holy Spirit needs our special function so He can fulfill His. Everything we made can serve salvation. The Holy Spirit can employ every choice the Son of God makes on his behalf. In darkness our specialness appears to be attack. But in the light we will see it as our special function in the plan to save the Son of God from all attack. He will understand he is safe, as he has always been in both time and eternity. This function has been given us for each other. Let us take it gently from one another's hand. If we do this one thing then salvation will be perfectly fulfilled in both of us.

We can be reborn and given new life again every instant. The Son of God's holiness gives life to us. He cannot die because his sinlessness is known to God. It cannot be sacrificed by us. We do not have the power to make of God and His Son what God did not Will. We cannot make our eyes and ears bear witness to the death of God and His Son. God's Son is not imprisoned in a body in Heaven. He is not sacrificed in solitude to sin. As he is in Heaven, so must he be eternally and everywhere. He is the same forever, born again each instant. He is untouched by time and beyond the sacrifice of life or death. He did not make either one. Only life was given him by One Who knows His gifts can never suffer sacrifice and loss.

We will stand in a holy place that sin has vacated when we see our brother as sinless. The face of Christ will be seen rising in its place. When we see the face of Christ we will recall our Father as He really is. Heaven's altar will rise and tower far above the world and reach beyond the universe to touch the Heart of all creation. The holiest of altars will be set where once we believed we looked on sin. Every light of Heaven will come here, to be rekindled and increased in joy. What was lost will be restored to them. Their radiance will be made whole again.

A world that will become an altar to the truth will rise where sin once was perceived. We will join the lights of Heaven there and sing their song of gratitude and praise. They will come to us to be complete and we will go with them. No one can hear the song of Heaven and remain without a voice that adds its power to the song, making it sweeter still. Each one will join the singing at the altar that was raised on the tiny spot that sin proclaimed to be its own. What was tiny will soar into a mighty chorus of song in which the universe has joined with a single voice.

The Son of God is as free as God created him. He was reborn the instant he chose to die. Forgive him now. He made an error in the past that God does not remember because it is not there. We shift back and forth between the past and present. Sometimes the past seems to be the present. We hear voices from the past and then doubt we heard them. We are like one who hallucinates and then doubts what he perceives. This is the borderland between the worlds, the bridge between past and present. The shadow of the past remains, but a light, dimly seen, is recognized. This light can never be forgotten. It draws us from the past into the present, where we really are.

It is natural to use the power God has given us as He would have it used. It is not arrogant to be as He created us, or to make use of what He gave to answer all His Son's mistakes and set him free. It is arrogant to lay aside the power He gave and choose a little senseless wish instead. God's gift to us is without limit. It can answer any circumstance. All problems can be resolved within its gracious light.

We are all holy because we have the Voice for God in each of us, calling to our brother to awaken the same Voice in him. When the Voice in him answers our call, we will receive salvation from him. It was there waiting for us to give it to him. God resides in him regardless of our attempts to condemn him, as He does in us. Let us look lovingly on our brother who has Christ within him so we can see his glory. Our brother carries Christ to us so our sins can be forgiven. But a shadow stands between our brother and ourselves, obscuring the face of Christ and memory of God. We do not want to trade Them for an ancient hate.

Their Presence will lift holiness back up on its ancient throne. What was a place of death will become a living temple, in a world of light, because of Them. They will undo what hate has made. We will stand on ground so holy Heaven leans to join with it. The shadow of an ancient hate will be gone. The land is no longer devastated where They have come.

Time is nothing to Them, its purpose is fulfilled when They have come. When They come, what never was passes to nothingness; what was given to hatred is claimed by love, and freedom sheds its light on every living thing. As each one comes home to Heaven the lights grow brighter because Heaven's own are returning. Heaven has been waiting a long time for this gift and is grateful. They come to gather in Their Own. The locked door is open. The light of Heaven shines on the world.

Let us practice the holy instant and be healed. Everything in the holy instant will be brought with us when we return to this world. Being blessed, we will give blessing. We are given life there to give to the dying world. The eyes of those who suffer will shine from the heart in thanks to us when we give blessing. The holy instant's radiance will light our eyes. They will be given sight to see beyond all suffering. They will see Christ's face instead. Healing will replace suffering. If we perceive healing, then suffering cannot be there. What we see, the world will observe, and will attest to.

When We Wake Our Brother

We cannot wake ourselves from our dream. But we can let ourselves be wakened. We can overlook our brother's dreams and forgive him his illusions. When we offer complete forgiveness, he will become our savior in our dream. When we see him shining in the space of light where God waits in the darkness, we will see that God Himself is where his body is. The body will disappear before this light. . The coming of the light means the darkness is gone. We will see our brother in glory and understand what really fills the gap so long perceived as keeping us apart. He will be given the power to forgive our illusions. Our gift of freedom will be given back to us.

When we forgive our brother on earth, the darkness can be lifted from his mind. And he will not forget his savior. He will keep our face beside him as he walks through darkness to the everlasting Light. We are holy because the Son of God can be our savior. He will come eagerly out of the shadows and shine on us in gratitude and love. The light will become brighter in both of us as the spark in the dream glows with our combined love. When we help him waken and make sure his waking eyes rest on us, we will be saved as he is.

We do not know what our brother is for because our function is obscure to us. We should not assign a role to him that we think will bring us happiness. We should not try to hurt him when he fails to take the part we assigned to him. He asks for help in every dream he has. We can give him help if we see the function of the dream as the Holy Spirit does. He can use every dream to serve the function given Him. Each dream becomes an offering of love because He loves the dreamer, not the dream. At its center is His Love for us, which lights everyone with love.

Our joint inheritance is remembered together and accepted by both of us. It is denied to both of us alone. Those who would be in control walk a lonely road. It should be clear that while we insist on leading or following we think we walk alone. This is the road to nowhere. The light cannot be given while we walk alone, so we cannot see the way. Beside us is the One Who holds the light before us. A blindfold can obscure our sight, but cannot darken the way.

Salvation cannot come in the dream while we are dreaming it. We think idols must be in it to save us from what we believe we have done that is sinful and has put out the inner light. But the light is still there. We are little children, only dreaming and idols are the toys we dream we play with. Children need toys. They pretend they rule the world. They give their toys the power to think and speak and move. But all this is in the minds of those who play with them. They forget they made the dream and the wishes they ascribe to the toys are really their own.

God's Thoughts are changeless, shining forever like a star that shines forever in an eternal sky. We are thoughts in the Mind of God. The Thought He holds of us is set so high in Heaven that it is unknown to those outside of Heaven. It was always there and will shine throughout eternity. Who knows the Father knows this light. Its purity does not depend on whether it is seen on earth or not. When we seek after idols we cannot know of this light.

The Light is in Each of Us

As we learn, we will make many concepts of the self. Each one will show the changes in our relationships as our perception of ourselves changes. The learning of the world loosens its grasp on our mind with each shift. It will eventually go, finally leaving our mind at peace.

We learn from the world that we are only images. But a time will come when images have gone and we do not know what we are. Our mind will be open and will allow truth to enter in. Truth is revealed when all concepts of the self have been cast aside. When every concept has been looked on with doubt, then the underlying assumptions will not stand in the light, and truth is free to return.

The concept we made of the self stands between us and the truth. We dimly see only images that we have made. The dark shadows we see are born in our imagination and come from our concepts that are based in fear. We see hell because fear is hell. But we have been given the vision and the inner Guide that will lead us out of this hell. Our loved ones will be beside us when we are released from the misery of this world.

While we wish to stay in hell we cannot be the savior of the Son of God. We can look on holiness only through holy eyes, expecting to see innocence everywhere. They call out the innocence in everyone they look on, expecting to see it. The innocent brings the light to everything he looks upon.

The light has been given to each of us. We must not hide it from the world, which needs it to shine away the darkness. Our brothers despair because we withhold the savior's vision and what they see is death. Their savior stands, mute, and looking at them with closed eyes. They cannot see until he looks on them with seeing eyes. He must offer them forgiveness with his own. We cannot be tempted not to listen when God Himself asks us to release His Son. It is us for whom He asks release.

"Light is the first of painters. There is no object so foul that intense light will not make it beautiful."

--Ralph Waldo Emerson

Chapter 11

THE FINAL JUDGEMENT

Introduction

Everyone is seeking the peace of God, either consciously or subconsciously. The Father calls His Son to return to Him and complete Him. What we have made here to indulge our desire for specialness will not give peace, just the opposite. When we consciously decide we do not like this state of hopelessness, then we will want to return to our natural state of complete happiness. To do this we will have to accept the task of reversing our thought system. It is not necessary to spend years in contemplative meditation or self-denial. All that is required is the willingness to let the Holy Spirit make all judgements for us and accept His guidance for every decision.

The way back to God is simple – we have to place ourselves in the service of the Holy Spirit. We will become the teachers of God then and dedicate our minds, tongues, feet and hands to this work. We do not have to preach, just know that the whole world is one in our holiness. Those who are sent to us will learn from our example. We will have to learn to love like God loves us – we will have to learn to love all our brothers and love them equally.

Some Answers

In Chapter 1, several questions were raised about our existence in this world. While it is impossible to understand the world of the ego, here are some explanations using the inadequate symbols of the human language. When we accept these teachings, which come from our elder brother, we will have answers to questions that have troubled philosophers throughout the ages.

What's it all About?

It is all about the Son of God being splintered into a multitude of individual selves, housed in bodies with their own private little worlds. God created us as a thought in His Mind, perfect as His only Son. In our creation God gave us all power in the universe, which we share with Him. He gave us free will. But we wanted special favor so we could pursue sin and indulge ourselves in special relationships. We made a world of getting and taking, with no thought of sharing with our brothers.

But we made a terrible mistake in our misuse of the power God gave us. When we made this dream world we did not give ourselves an easy way to escape back to our natural condition as a thought of God. Our power is so great we were able to make a believable world with believable illusions and believable rules of the game we wanted to play.

It is an upside-down world where we love to hate and hate to love. It is a world of little children who love to see wars and disasters of every kind played out. It is a dream world where God is kept away from His separated Son. The Son of

God wanders this world bereft of his powers, miserable and believing he is helpless while obeying the dictates of the ego, which he made. Most of our real thoughts, those that we think with God, are buried underneath an insane stream of body thoughts that are based on judgement and hate, thinly disguised as kindness and "love." But the mind, when it is isolated from the body, cannot make mistakes like these.

That is why we are still able to act in a decent way toward our brother despite the shrill cries of the ego directing us to attack him. However, we are condemned to stay in this world we have made until we can transcend the ego entirely by changing our mind about who we are. We will continue to exist in an ancient instant over and over again until we find our way out of it.

Everyone has a burning, subconscious desire to return to our Father, Who we have a deep and abiding love for. But we have buried the memory of Him beneath a mad barrage of childish toys that we invented. These toys frighten us with their apparent intent to harm us. But we continue to play with them, heedless, as little children are, of the harm we are doing to God's Son.

Why Am I Here?

The world we see represents our thoughts projected on the canvas of the world we made. It shows us a picture of attack on everything and everyone. The instant we made this world of splintered little selves, God placed His Answer to the separation in our minds – the Holy Spirit. He is the Voice of our conscience, the fountain from which springs all of our better impulses. If we are willing to let Him be our Guide, He will use our body and this world as training devices to correct the errors in our minds. The world we see is the result of the errors in our minds. Our purpose here is to return to our home in God. We will return when we step back and let the Holy Spirit lead the way.

We have real thoughts that we think with God as well as insane ones. The Holy Spirit will teach us to let our real thoughts show us the real world. We share our real thoughts with everyone because minds are joined. Our real thoughts will awaken the real thoughts in everyone and the real world will dawn on everyone's sight.

Our function here is to see the world through our holiness. The whole world will be blessed by us because our holiness can accomplish anything. Our forgiveness will lead to the end of suffering and despair. No one will need to sacrifice anything because everything will be shared in a world where there is only happiness and love. Our task is to let the Holy Spirit reverse our thinking about ourselves and this world. For Him to accomplish this, we must keep no secrets from Him and be willing to forgive ourselves and our brothers for the errors we thought were made. In reality these errors never happened, because we see what we want to see as we project our thoughts from our mind onto our brothers.

The Holy Spirit will teach us to feel the Love of God within so we can look on the world and see it in a new light. We will see the world shining in its innocence. It will be alive with hope and blessed with love. He will teach us that the peace of God is the only peace possible. It will be ours when we feel the Love of God within. This is one of the most important lessons in *A Course in Miracles®* – we must put everything we taught ourselves aside and place ourselves under the Holy

Spirit's guidance. Ask Him about every decision to be made. That is why we are here.

What Am I?

We think we are a body, limited by the body's capabilities and shortcomings. We think the mind is housed in the body and so can be harmed if the body is harmed. But the mind is unlimited forever, beyond the laws of time and space and with the strength and power to do whatever it is asked. It was created by Love and rests in God.

A tiny part of the mind is occupied by something we made – the ego. Another part is occupied by something God put there – the Holy Spirit. There is a constant stream of messages coming from both that give us guidance on how we should conduct our lives. The raucous shrieks of the ego drown out the Holy Spirit if we let them. We will govern our actions according to the dictates of the ego if that is the voice we choose to listen to. If we refuse to listen to the ego and ask the Holy Spirit for guidance before we make any decisions, we will be well set on the path back to God.

Our true nature is spiritual. We are not an image living in a decaying body in a dream world full of hate, fear, misery and suffering. We are the Sons of God, a part of God's Mind and He is part of our mind. We are the holy home of God Himself. As part of His Mind, we are sinless. We live in eternity, not in time. When the Holy Spirit has finished using the body for our training, it will be gently laid aside. Our true life will continue on, for we are immortal.

Each of us is writing the script for everything that happens to us, moment by moment. We surround ourselves with the environment we want to experience. In the center of this environment is the image we have made of what we want to be. We want this image protected and given pleasure by the environment that is seen through the image's eyes and experienced by the other senses of the body. The image sends out these messengers with specific instructions to return with messages that agree with what the image wants to experience.

But the part of our mind that controls these messengers – the ego – hates us. It does everything possible to make our life miserable without our becoming aware that it is doing all this to us. Our reality is our oneness with the Sonship and with God. The Sonship is one in all respects. Oneness cannot be divided. God's Will is that His Son be united with Him in His Oneness. If we choose to go astray, the Holy Spirit can bring us back to where God and His Son wait for our recognition. Together they give us the gift of oneness which will eliminate the separation as we return to our Father.

God holds us all within Him as one. He proclaims the Oneness of Himself and His Son through His Teacher. If we are silent, learn to keep the ego's voice quiet and listen, we will hear the miracle of oneness He teaches. We will begin to experience the feeling of oneness when we learn to separate out a single second and experience it as timeless.

To be alone is to be guilty and to deny the Oneness of the Father and the Son. The Holy Spirit sees only oneness where the ego perceives one person as a replacement for another. Heaven is an awareness of perfect oneness. There is nothing outside this oneness and nothing else within.

What am I?

I am the holy, sinless Son of God Himself.

If we keep repeating this to ourselves then we will be saving time on our journey back to God.

Is There a Better Way?

Of course there is a better way than this uncertain existence where we never get any satisfaction when one of the many goals we have set for ourselves is reached. That way is now clear. It is to return to our Father in His Heaven which is our natural home. Once returned to our natural state, we will be filled with joy. Everyone and everything will look beautiful in our sight, which will be transformed into the vision of Christ. This will transpire when we accept the Atonement for ourselves.

The Atonement is a chain of miracles and forgiveness that will end in our salvation. And salvation is a promise God has made that we will all return to Him eventually. All paths lead to God and our task is to stay on the shortest one. This path will be pointed out to us by the Holy Spirit if we ask Him.

First, we must see our brothers as sinless. We must see the world through our holiness and give everyone our blessing. To do this it is necessary to relinquish all judgement. Judgement is the same as condemnation; they are responsible for all the sorrows of this world.

Next, we must give our unholy relationships to the Holy Spirit for His purposes of holiness. As the relationship develops into a holy relationship we must continue to let ourselves be guided by the Holy Spirit. We must ask Him to teach us how to forgive. Then we must give our complete forgiveness to every living thing. The Holy Spirit represents a state of mind so close to One-mindedness, perception can be carried over to knowledge. This final step is taken by God.

Our goal is to see the real world. When we reach it, God will reach down and carry us across the bridge that connects the real world to Heaven, where we belong. Our joy will be unlimited when we have returned to our natural home. We will be surrounded by peace, joy, unconditional love and happiness.

What is Love?

The reality of the world *is* love. The Holy Spirit will teach us how to replace every fearful thought with a loving thought. He will show us that a fearful thought is an appeal for love. He will exchange our nightmares for happy dreams of love. Happy dreams will lead to knowledge, which only waits for our welcome. All that is required is a little willingness on our part.

Love is limitless, it is everywhere. Our goal should be to love our brother as we love ourselves and to love ourselves as we love our brother. We should love all our brothers and equally, just as our Father does. We can become aware of love if we make the effort to perceive our brother's loving thoughts *and* his appeals for help. We must accept only his loving thoughts and look at all else as an appeal for help. Let us remember that when a brother attacks us, it is a call for love.

The sick do not love themselves. To heal ourselves, we must love ourselves. We deny to ourselves the love that would heal us because we are afraid of it. Just as we recognize the call for love in hatred, sickness also is a call for love. The Holy Spirit's Love is our strength. His promise is: "Seek and we *will* find." We can put our complete trust in Him because He will never deceive God's Son. He loves him with the Love of the Father.

We cannot learn of perfect love with the lower part of our split mind. We think we love and yet we seem to lose what we love. This is an insane belief because love cannot be lost. God's Son is not guilty, he deserves only love for he gives only love. He was created out of Love and he lives in love. He is an extension of and extends the Love of his Father

We do not want the separation healed because the veil hiding our love for the Father would be gone and we would gladly ascend into Heaven. But we resist this because we are afraid of God. We are afraid we would lose the "life" we have made here. We could no longer play with the toys we have made here in this world.

Beneath the ego's foundation, and much stronger than it, is our intense and burning love of God, and His for us. In our secret place we call for love to our Father, as He calls us to Himself.

Our real power lies in love. We think our hatred is our strength, but that is wrong. If we truly heard the call of love we could not control our joy. The whole world we made would disappear. So we are afraid of God's Love. We think it would sweep away our world and reduce us to nothingness. We would rather embrace the insane ego-world we made than love, which we did not.

If we exclude one brother from our love, we hide a secret place in our mind where the Holy Spirit is not welcome. We cannot have real relationships with any of God's Sons unless we love them all and equally. The only way to look within and see the light of love is to love our brother and release him from guilt as we would be released. We who have always loved the Father can not be afraid to look within because love is guiltless. We will see no guilt within, only the shining Love of our Father.

The real world will come to us because we love it. Love always leads to love. This place is in us and Love will lead us there if we seek it. Love is the emotion given to us, the others we made. The world we see through love is Christ's vision. His vision is His gift of love to us, given to Him by the Father for us. Awaking to Christ is giving love of our own free will. Those who accept our love hold it out to us in return. We have followed the laws of love even in our sleep, for Christ has protected us. Although God's Son slept, he is still as loving as his Father.

Love is not special. If we single out part of the Sonship for our love then we impose guilt on all our relationships and they become unreal. We should not try to love differently than God does because we can love only as He loves. There is no love apart from His. We will have no idea what love is like until we recognize this.

God watches over His Son so nothing will touch him except God Himself. God placed him in Himself where there is no pain; only love surrounding him without end. God goes with us wherever we go. His Presence watches over us and protects us always.

We cannot wake ourselves, but we can let ourselves be wakened. If we ignore our brother's dreams and forgive him his illusions, he will become our savior from our dreams. As we see him shining in the light where God lives in the darkness we made, we will see that God Himself is where we thought we saw his body. The body will disappear before this light. Whom we forgive will be given the power to forgive us our illusions. Our gift of freedom will be given back to us.

We did not make love but we can extend it to every living thing. This is how we forgive our brothers here on earth, so the darkness can be lifted from our mind. When our forgiveness has brought him light, he will not forget his savior, because that would leave him still in hell. He will want to keep our face, where he saw the light, beside him as he walks through darkness to the everlasting Light.

We are holy because the Son of God can be our savior. He comes eagerly out of the shadows and shines on us in gratitude and love. We share the light our Father gave us with him. It will be brighter because we gave our light to him. The light in us will become as bright as the light shining in him. This is the spark that shines in the dream. We can help him waken and be sure that when he wakes his eyes will rest on us. We will be savior to each other.

What is Death?

Death is nothing, an attempt to resolve conflict by not deciding at all. Death is made by the ego. *It will not work.* All sickness and death we think we see reflect our state of mind. If we think we are a body, then we will be afraid of death. But there is no death, only a belief in death. This world is left by truth, not by death.

Death is the result of the thought we call the ego. Life is the result of the Thought of God. And ideas do not leave their source. Sin, guilt and death all come from the ego. They oppose life and innocence and the Will of God Himself. Such opposition can only reside in the sick minds of the insane. God does not know of sin and its results.

Some may ask; Does death follow automatically because there is life? The answer is: If there was a past life ending in death, it must have been futile if it needs death to prove it had an existence. But we do not question this. However, we do question the existence of Heaven. It seems obvious that Heaven would be more desirable than death.

There is nothing outside ourselves. We re-enact a wasted life of separation and loss of power in this world again and again. The world is a canvas on which we are constantly painting our idea of what life should be like according to the dictates of the ego. The ego makes useless attempts at making amends in this life for injuries inflicted on our brothers. Everything eventually decays in the painting so the final strokes of the brush lead to death. We repeat this process endlessly until we voluntarily give it up by working out our salvation in the present.

The Son of God is reborn each instant until he chooses not to die again. He chooses death in every wish to hurt instead of what his Father wills for him. But every instant offers life to him. His Father wills that he should live and return to Him.

There is no life outside of Heaven, only illusions in conflict. They seem lifelike at their best. At their worst they seem like death. Both states are judgements on what is not life. The conflict of illusions is perceived as a blockage in our path which keeps us from Heaven. But illusions are only forms. Their content is never believable.

The ego's belief in what is real makes it appear that God's Will is outside ourselves where It conflicts with ours. But God would not deprive us of what we want. We cannot live apart from Him even in time. What He created can sleep and dream but cannot die because He created us immortal. God's Son cannot will death for himself. God neither Wills death for us, nor do we.

The Holy Spirit teaches that we have eternal life. If we treasure death, we pay a heavy price for it. We will sell everything else to purchase it. But we cannot sell our inheritance – the Kingdom of Heaven – for we are part of God and He is whole.

The Holy Spirit's teaching will eliminate guilt if we choose to listen. We feel guilty because we think subconsciously we have been treacherous to God. We listen to the ego's voice which tells us that we deserve death because of our treachery. Confusing ourselves with the ego, we think we want death. We think death comes from God, not the ego.

The ego believes our existence is all about destruction and death. It thinks our only inheritance is the dust out of which we were made. If it is reasonably satisfied with us, it offers oblivion. If not, it offers us hell. The ego's followers do not realize they have pledged themselves to death. They are offered freedom by the Holy Spirit but do not accept it.

The waste that time seems to bring is due to our identification with the ego. The ego uses time to convince us of the inevitability of death. It does not realize that the death of the body would be its end. The Holy Spirit uses time to teach us of the inevitability of life, which has no end.

The ego hates us and wants us dead, but not itself. It does not want us to have peace even in death. It believes it can pursue us beyond the grave, offering immortality in hell. It allies itself with time but is not time's friend. It tells us Heaven is not for us because of our guilt. Guilt will be gone when the belief in sin is gone. Death will be gone when the ego is silenced..

If we let the ego be our guide then the belief in hell will be one of our guidelines and we will be afraid of death. The ego's goal is hell, teaching us that hell is in our future. It does not believe what it teaches – death and dissolution. It wants us to think of death as an end to pain, so we will welcome it. But if we do, we will never understand that there is no death.

The strange devotion to death is a dark shadow that falls over all living things. The fear of death is really its attraction. It has no hold except on those who seek it out. But *no one can die unless he chooses death.* When we are tempted to yield to the desire for death, we should remember that our elder brother did not die.

Those who fear death do not see how often and loudly they call for it. They ask it to come and save them from communication with the Sonship and with God. They are afraid to communicate for fear they would find love. Death is seen as safety, the savior from the light, answer to the Answer and the silencer of God's Voice. Retreating to death does not end conflict. Only God's Answer is the end.

The fear of death will yield to love's real attraction. Without the fear of death we would remember our Father. The belief in death holds up the darkest veil over the face of Christ. The dedication to death is only the promise, made to the ego, never to lift this veil. It is our promise never to let union call us out of separation. *It is the fear of God.*

Let us ask ourselves: Do we like what we have made? A world of danger, murder and attack, where we wind our timid way, alone and frightened. The most we hope for is that death will wait a little longer before it claims us and we disappear. *We made all this up.* It reflects what we think we are. It is how we see ourselves.

Perhaps we do not see the role forgiveness plays in ending death and all beliefs rising from guilt Our savior, standing next to us, offers salvation when forgiven by us. He offers death when we condemn him. We see in everyone the reflection of what we choose to have him be to us. If we decide against his proper function, we deprive him of the joy he would have found by fulfilling the role God gave him. Heaven is not lost to him alone. It can only be regained if we show him the way. And we will find it, walking at his side.

There is a risk of thinking death is peace. But death is opposite to peace because it is opposite to life. Life is peace. Let us awaken and forget all thoughts of death. We will find the peace of God is with us.

What is Life?

Forgiveness is the answer to any attack. Hate is answered in the name of love. It has been given us to save the Son of God from crucifixion, hell and death. We have the power to save the Son of God because his Father willed it be so. All salvation lies in our hands. Love can enter only where fear is gone. Fear is gone when we place the future in the Hands of God.

Life is of the mind and in the mind; life is peace. God is the Giver of life. Only what communicates with God can have life. The Last Judgement is really the doorway to life because no one who lives in fear is really alive. When we fear salvation, we are choosing death, darkness and perception instead of life, light and knowledge. Death is the result of the thought we call the ego. Life is the result of the Thought of God, and ideas do not leave their source.

In the little time between life and death, we think we have some time when we can be alone, where everyone conflicts with us. We think we can choose the road that leads away from conflict and difficulties that are not our concern. But they *are* our concern. We cannot escape from them. We will take with us what must go with us whatever road we choose to walk along.

When our body, the ego and dreams are gone, we will last forever. This is not accomplished through death because the body neither lives nor dies, it is neutral. We can overcome death the same as our elder brother did because we share the same Mind he does.

Health is the natural state of everything when interpreted by the Holy Spirit. It is the result of ending all attempts to use the body for purposes other than love. Health happens when all attack thoughts are given up. It is the beginning of the proper perspective of life under His guidance. The Holy Spirit uses time to teach us of the inevitability of life, which has no end. We will renounce death, and exchange it for life when we accept the Holy Spirit's purpose as our own.

The Holy Spirit teaches that we have eternal life. We were given the gift of life and it is ours to give. But in this world we do not give it because we are not extending life by seeing only our immortal brothers. We look about and see our brothers in corruptible bodies instead of seeing the Great Rays shining from them. When we learn to look within and see our elder brother we will realize that the Father gave us eternal life. Then we will look out upon a world that cannot die.

We constantly wage a war against ourselves. We started it to teach the Son of God he is not himself, that he is not his Father's Son. We lost the memory of the Father so we could reach this goal. It is forgotten as long as we think we are a body. What we gave "life" to is not really alive. It only symbolizes our wish to be alive independently from life; alive in death. Death is perceived as life and living as death. But there is no death, only life exists. The world we know is based on all this confusion.

There is no life outside of Heaven, only illusions in conflict. The conflict of illusions is perceived as a barrier to Heaven. But illusions are only forms. Their content is never true.

The body can become a symbol of life and a breath of immortality. If we let it have healing as its purpose. Then it will send out a healing message to everyone. We should let the body have no purpose that comes from the past. When it shines in obvious good health and happiness for all to see it will proclaim the truth and the value of belief in the Love of the Father it represents. Everyone who perceives it will be healed.

The Last Judgement

What we see in this world is what we project here. If we have judged ourselves as damned, we will see the world as damned. If we see disaster and catastrophe, then we tried to crucify the Son of God. If we see holiness and hope, we have joined the Will of God in trying to set him free. These are the only choices we can make. We will recognize which one we made by what we see and hear. As soon as we have accepted the Atonement for ourselves, we will see God's Son as guiltless. If we look upon him as guiltless, we will see his oneness.

It is foolish to try to judge what we could see behind the closed doors in our mind. We do not have to imagine what the world is really like. We can be shown which doors are open. We can see which way leads to light and safety, and which leads to darkness. We do not have to guess. Vision will always show us where to go, but judgement will always give us false directions.

We cannot understand that our own Creator did not lay a judgement on His Son. We want to deny Him His own children. But they have never been denied by Him. His Son could never be condemned for what he dreamt. Our remembering only witnesses to the fear of God. He has not done the thing we fear. Neither have we. We have not lost our innocence.

Nothing the Son of God believes can be destroyed. What is truth to him must be brought to the last comparison he will ever make – the final judgement on this world. It is the judgement of truth on illusion, of knowledge on perception. This world has no meaning and does not exist. In this world it is not clear what is the same and what is different.

God's final judgement will come only when it is no longer associated with fear. When everyone welcomes it, it will be given. The Son of God will hear his innocence proclaimed around the world, setting it free.

"This is God's Final Judgement : 'You are still my holy Son, forever innocent, forever loving and forever loved, as limitless as your Creator, and completely changeless and forever pure. Therefor, awaken and return to Me. I am your Father and you are My Son.'"

A Course in Miracles ®

EPILOGUE

We are all strangers here. We will all return to God eventually, which is our natural state, for that is God's plan. Once the journey back to God is begun, the end is certain. Some will do it through years of denial and meditation. Most have to repeat the errors of this world over and over again until they find their way. But the quickest way is through *A Course in Miracles®*.

The teachings in *The Sons of God* are my interpretation of the marvelous concepts in the Course. I wrote this book in the belief there was a need for a simplified explanation of some of the more abstract ideas in the Course. The Course is designed to be self-teaching but most find a group helpful in discussing the principles.

I recommend you obtain a copy of the Course for your further studies. You can probably find one at the bookstore in the Unity Church nearest you. Local classes in the Course are usually conducted at Unity Churches. They will welcome your inquiry and participation. If there is no Unity Church near you, you can obtain your own copy of the Course from:

Miracle Distribution Center
1141 East Ash Ave.,
Fullerton, CA 92831-5095

1-800-359-ACIM(2246)

The Foundation for Inner Peace maintains a directory of study groups. They may be reached at;

http://www.acim.org
6 Venado Dr.
Tiburon, CA 94920

NOTES

NOTES

NOTES

NOTES

NOTES

NOTES

NOTES

NOTES

NOTES

NOTES

NOTES

NOTES

NOTES

ORDER FORM

ORDER

Please send the following books:

I understand that I may return any book for a full refund, no questions asked.

Qty (.......) The Sons of God @ $12.95

TOTAL Books (.............) + tax (........) + shipping (.........)

PLEASE PRINT CLEARLY

Name ....

Address..

City..State.........Zip.................

Telephone (..........)..

Sales Tax: Florida residents please add appropriate sales tax.

Shipping: Book rate - $3.00 for the first book, 75 cents for each additional. Priority mail - $4.00 per book.

Payment: Make checks payable to:
Love Publishing.

Send to: P.O. Box 611
Indiantown, FL 34956

ORDER FORM

ORDER

Please send the following books:

I understand that I may return any book for a full refund, no questions asked.

Qty (.......) The Sons of God @ $12.95

TOTAL Books (.............) + tax (........) + shipping (.........)

PLEASE PRINT CLEARLY

Name ....

Address...

City...State..........Zip.................

Telephone (..........)...

Sales Tax: Florida residents please add appropriate sales tax.

Shipping: Book rate - $3.00 for the first book, 75 cents for each additional. Priority mail - $4.00 per book.

Payment: Make checks payable to:
Love Publishing.

Send to: P.O. Box 611
Indiantown, FL 34956